STRONG FAITH

An introduction to the study of God

David L. Parker

CROSSBOOKS
PUBLISHING

CrossBooks™
A Division of LifeWay
One LifeWay Plaza
Nashville, TN 37234
www.crossbooks.com
Phone: 1-866-768-9010

Scripture quotations taken from the New American Standard Bible®, Copyright © 1960, 1962, 1963, 1968, 1971, 1972, 1973, 1975, 1977, 1995 by The Lockman Foundation. Used by permission." (www.Lockman.org)

First published by CrossBooks 8/22/2014

ISBN: 978-1-4627-5193-8 (sc)
ISBN: 978-1-4627-5195-2 (hc)
ISBN: 978-1-4627-5194-5 (e)

Library of Congress Control Number: 2014915115

Printed in the United States of America.

"Yet, with respect to the promise of God, he did not waver in unbelief but grew strong in faith, giving glory to God," -Romans 4:20

For my sweetest friend.

Table of Contents

Table of Contents Continued

Table of Contents Continued

Table of Contents Continued

Introduction

It is my desire to see Christians grow strong in their faith. Our faith should be robust and unwavering.

But how can our faith be strong when we have a limited understanding of the object of our faith?

Romans 10:17 instructs us that "...*faith comes from hearing, and hearing by the word of Christ.*" God's word informs our faith, revealing God in all His glory.

In the Bible, we learn many great faith building truths. But we often struggle to connect these individual truths to form an accurate and clear understanding of God.

What we do comprehend, we can have difficulty retaining. It is as if the truths presented in the Bible lay unconnected in a mental inbox, forgotten and dust covered.

What if you could arrange the truths that you have learned from the Bible and see how they relate to each other?

Theology is like a bulletin board to organize the truths you learn from the Bible. Theology provides the framework to help you organize your thoughts and better understand God's Person, character and works.

With a theological framework, these biblical truths will now be connected in your understanding and relevant to your soul. The result will be a deeper, more intimate understanding of God that you can lean on all your days.

Connecting together the truths you learn about God and His relations to the universe will strengthen your faith and thrill your heart. With this in mind, I wrote the following theological primer.

Introduction Continued

This book is loosely based on Augustus Strong's <u>Systematic Theology</u>. Strong's <u>Systematic Theology</u> has been a great influence on theological study and Baptist thought since its introduction in the late nineteenth century. It was my most cherished textbook when I was a student many years ago at Southeastern Baptist Theological Seminary.

I have found Strong's work immensely rewarding in my own faith and devotion. However, it is not an easy volume to navigate. Many readers may find it lengthy and dense.

Strong's work was written for the academic, complete with small print, arcane references, and extensive footnotes.

This book has a different intended audience. It is written for the laity. It is intended for personal study and devotion.

Each chapter is meant to be a clear explanation of a truth about God that is easy to grasp and faith affirming.

These truths complement one another to build up your faith and knowledge of God.

I pray that this book will not only increase your knowledge of God, but your devotion to Him as well.

The clearer you see God, the closer you will desire to be with Him and seek to honor Him in all you do.

May you grow strong in faith and bring glory to God.

Gain Christ! (Philippians 3:8),

David L. Parker

Tequesta, FL

I.   INTRODUCTION TO THEOLOGY

Chapter 1

Definition of Theology

Theology is the science of God and of the relations between God and the universe.

- Theology is not just the study of God.
- Nor is it only the study of God and His relation to man.
- It also accounts for the relation of God to the universe.

Theology is the study of God. It is the study of God's Person. It is the study of God's nature. It is the study of God's attributes. It is the effort to know and understand God.

Theology also attempts to understand God's relation to all that He has created. God is known by the way He relates to mankind. God is known through His governance of all His creation. We know Him through His works and activities.

Theology gives account of those relations between God and the universe in view of which we speak of Creation, Providence and Redemption. These are His primary works.

Theology gives account of these works and activities so far as they come within our knowledge. They are the basis of our knowledge of God (Ps. 77:11-12).

Theology has been called the "science of the sciences". Theology has this title, not in the sense of including all these sciences, but in the sense of explaining their results. Only by the study of God are we provided with the underlying ground and foundation of these other sciences (Ps. 36:9).

"You will seek me and find me when you seek me with all your heart." –Jeremiah 29:13

All other sciences require theology for their complete explanation. Only when we consider the relation of finite things to God does the study of them throw true light on God's character (Ps. 111:1-4).

> *The LORD is near to all who call upon Him, to all who call upon Him in truth.*
> **–Psalm 145:18**

Everyone has a theology or belief about God. But that does not mean that everyone's theology is proper or correct. We must wrestle with our beliefs to conform them to God's reality. This effort is one of the most rewarding endeavors that we can undertake (2 Cor. 4:18).

When you court or date someone, you seek to learn about them. You want to find out all about them, what makes them act, what they like and dislike. You take pleasure in discovering new things about them. So should our hearts be toward God (Ps. 66:1-5, 16).

God invites us to learn about Him. Think about that for a moment. The God who created all things desires to relate to us! He wants us to know Him. But God wants us to get it right. God is jealous of His reputation. He wants us to know Him as He has revealed Himself. God wants us to worship Him in spirit and truth. God created us to have a relationship with Him. This is the purpose of theology.

Bible verses for devotion:

Genesis 3:8-9 –What is God really asking when He asks "Where are you?"

Romans 1:18-25– Is God concerned with our knowledge of Him? How so?

Romans 12:2 – How are we transformed?

Chapter 2

Aim of Theology

The aim of theology is to discover the facts respecting God and His relationship to all things, and then display these facts as connected parts that together reveal a clearer picture of God's Person and works.

- Theology does not create, but only discovers facts.
- It is necessary to arrange these facts and their relations.
- Our arrangement must reflect God's thoughts and order.

Theology discovers facts and relations, but it does not create them. The facts about God and His relationship to all things is the core of theology. These divine facts have an existence independent of the subjective thought of the theologian. They must be God's self-expression, not men's.

Science is more than the observing, recording, verifying and formulating of objective facts. Science seeks to recognize and explain the relations of these facts to each another. It seeks to unite the individual facts and relations into a true and comprehensive explanation of the whole.

Theology seeks to provide this framework on which to hang these various facts about God. It then seeks to display them in such a way as to show how they relate to each other and therefore present the clearest picture of God's Person and works. We strive to give an orderly account (Luke 1:3).

As theology deals with objective facts and their relations, the arrangement of these facts is not optional.

These facts require a framework. Scattered bricks and timbers are not a house. So too, scattered facts and their relations are not a theology. They must be fitted together.

In a court of law, facts are sought to explain a matter. It takes time and effort to establish

> *Jesus said to him,*
> *You shall love the*
> *Lord your God*
> *with all your heart,*
> *and with all your*
> *soul, and with*
> *all your mind.*
> **–Matthew 22:37**

the facts of the case and demonstrate how they relate to one another. The end result hopefully presents the truth accurately (2 Tim. 2:15; 1 Thes. 5:21).

This is also the aim of theology. We want to accurately present God's truth from the facts and their relations to the best of our ability. A good theologian thinks over again God's thoughts and brings them into God's order, as the builders of Solomon's temple took the stones already hewn, and fit them into the places for which the architect had designed them. We aim to display God and not ourselves (2 Cor. 4:5-6).

A good theologian works with a pencil. He realizes he is prone to error. Therefore, he is humble in his task and open to constant revision. The facts of God do not change. But our understanding and perception of them can change.

Theology requires great effort to discover the facts about God and arrange them in a way that best reflects God's thoughts and order. This is the aim of theology (Ps. 119:18).

Bible verses for devotion:

Jeremiah 9:23-24 –What are we to glory in? Wisdom, might and riches take time and discipline to acquire. Is knowing God worth the effort to you?

Chapter 3

Possibility of Theology

Theology is possible because of a threefold ground. First, God exists and relates to the universe. Second, He has given the human mind capacity to know Him. Third, He has revealed Himself to man.

- God exists.
- God created man to know Him.
- God communicates Himself to us through His revelation.

All science rests on faith. We have faith in our existence. We have faith in the existence of a world objective and external to us. We have faith in the existence of other persons than ourselves. We have faith in the trustworthiness of our faculties. But physical science is not invalidated by our faith. Indeed, it is faith that makes all science possible.

It is by faith that we know that God exists. If theology is to be thrown out because of this presupposition, then all other sciences must be thrown out with it.

Faith is knowledge. It is a larger and more fundamental sort of knowledge. Faith is not only a kind of knowing, but the highest kind of knowing. Faith is an operation of man's higher rational nature (Eph. 1:17-19).

Faith is distinct from our other senses and from our reasoning. But faith is never opposed to reasoning, only to our sight. As all true knowledge comes from God, our faith must be reasonable as it is truly the highest knowledge.

Faith is a knowledge conditioned by holy affection. Its only peculiarity as a cognitive sense is that is conditioned by holy affection.

> *...for he who comes to God must believe that He is, and that He is a rewarder of those who seek Him.*
> *–Hebrews 11:6*

God created man giving us the capacity to have a relationship with Him. Man's capacity to recognize and know God is practically inseparable from a holy love for God (Ps. 25:12, 14).

To have faith in God is to both know and love Him. We can't know God by intellect alone. The heart must go with the intellect to make knowledge of the divine things possible.

The faith which apprehends God's being and working is not opinion or imagination. Faith is certitude with regard to spiritual realities, upon the testimony of our rational nature and upon the testimony of God. Faith comes from God.

Therefore, faith can furnish, and only faith can furnish, fit and sufficient material for a true theology (2 Cor. 3:15-16).

In order for us to know God, He has revealed Himself to us. This self-revelation of God makes it possible for finite man to have a relationship with an infinite God.

This self-revelation of God makes up the material of theology. We will study His self-revelation in the remainder of this book.

Bible verses for devotion:

Hebrews 11:1-3 –What does this passage tell us about faith and knowledge?

1 Corinthians 2:6-16–What do these verses have to say about faith, knowledge and revelation?

Chapter 4

Necessity of Theology

Theology is a necessity because our minds crave order, our character needs a foundation to rest on, and our devotion and duty to God demands it.

• The human mind has an organizing instinct.
• Christian character rests on truth as its foundation.
• Theology is necessary to know God and glorify Him.

The human mind cannot endure confusion or apparent contradictions in known facts. Our minds by design crave order and seek to harmonize and unify knowledge. This is true in all areas of human inquiry, but it is peculiarly true of our knowledge of God (Eph. 3:17-19).

Theology is a rational necessity. Since truth in regards to God is the most important knowledge of all, theology meets the deepest want of man's rational nature (Mat. 4:4).

All knowledge of God exerts influence on one's character. A poorly informed theology will produce poor character in the church and its members. Godly character is a fruit which only grows from the tree of Christian theology (2 Pet. 3:18).

Truth thoroughly digested is essential to the growth of Christian character in individuals and in the church. Rather than deadening the affections, theology draws them out and stirs them up by connecting them to Christ. Right doctrine without a right walk is a tree without fruit. A right walk without right doctrine is a tree without roots (Col. 1:9-11).

Theology is a necessity for us to know God and make Him known to others. To know God and make Him known, we must know the facts with regard to God and their relations to each other.

In order to glorify God and make God known to others, we must present God correctly and vividly (Mat. 23:15). Nothing nullifies our efforts to make God known more than confusion and inconsistencies in our doctrines. This robs God of

As a result, we are no longer to be children, tossed here and there by waves and carried about by every wind of doctrine, by the trickery of men, by craftiness in deceitful scheming; but speaking the truth in love, we are to grow up in all aspects into Him who is the head, even Christ.
–Ephesians 4:14-15

His glory. To misrepresent or mutilate this knowledge is to not only sin against the Revealer, but also to harm another's faith (1 Tim. 1:3-7).

The best safeguard against this misrepresentation is diligent study of the doctrines of God, and especially its central theme, the Person and work of Jesus Christ.

Working out our theology brings order to our outlook. This effort richly rewards us with a foundation on which we can build Christian character. It also rewards us with a more intimate knowledge of God and a great ability to glorify Him.

Bible verses for devotion:

Colossians 1:9-11 –What does this passage teach us about the relation of theology to our character?

Luke 17:2–What does this mean in regard to our duty to faithfully and accurately make God known to others?

Chapter 5

Limitations of Theology

Theology does not give us an exhaustive knowledge of God and of the relations between God and the universe. A perfect system of theology is impossible. Theology has its limitations.

- Theology is limited by finite human understanding.
- Theology is limited by our knowledge of Scripture.
- Theology is limited in the silence of written revelation.
- Theology is limited by lack of spiritual discernment.
- Lack of discernment is caused by our moral imperfection.

God is infinite. Man is finite. There is a limit to our comprehension. Job 11:7 asks *"Can you discover the depths of God? Can you discover the limits of the Almighty?"*

Our understanding is both limited and imperfect. Because of the infinity and perfection of the divine nature, some things are incomprehensible and mysterious to man. Isa. 55:8-9 says *"For My thoughts are not your thoughts, nor are your ways My ways, declares the LORD. For as the heavens are higher than the earth, so are My ways higher than your ways, and My thoughts than your thoughts."*

Our limitations include our inability to reconcile apparent contradictions in Scripture. For example, we see God's sovereignty and human freedom, or Christ's divinity and Christ's humanity, respectively as two disconnected facts, when perhaps deeper insight would see but one.

Theology is further limited by the silence of written revelation. There are many questions not addressed in Scripture. We must wait to have these answered. 1 Cor. 13:12 says *"For now we see in a mirror, dimly..."*

> *Oh, the depth of the riches both of the wisdom and knowledge of God! How unsearchable are His judgments and unfathomable His ways!*
> **–Romans 11:33-34**

In heaven, this will be rectified. In 1 Cor. 13:10, Paul promises *"But when the perfect comes, the partial will be done away."*

Theology is also limited by our lack of spiritual discernment caused by sin. Romans 1:25 laments the sinners who *"... exchanged the truth of God for a lie, and worshiped and served the creature rather than the Creator..."*

As our love of God is a condition of religious knowledge, all moral imperfection in the individuals and in the church serves as a hindrance to our theology. In Mat. 5:8, Jesus said *"Blessed are the pure in heart, for they shall see God."*

Theology has its limitations. But these limitations should not discourage us. What we can know, we must cling to and cherish.

Deuteronomy 29:29 promises us that *"The secret things belong to the LORD our God, but the things revealed belong to us and to our sons forever, that we may observe all the words of this law."*

Bible verses for devotion:

John 3:3– What is prerequisite of our religious knowledge?

1 Cor. 13:12– When will our knowledge be perfected?

[handwritten margin note: we may not get answers to our questions. But if we trust in God, one day, we will.]

II. MATERIAL OF THEOLOGY

Chapter 6

General Revelation

General revelation is the concept that God reveals Himself to man as the Creator. All of creation is like a mirror that reflects the existence and glory of God. General revelation reveals God as Creator, but not as Redeemer.

- General revelation reveals God's existence to all men.
- General revelation reveals God to man's conscience.
- General revelation renders man without excuse.
- General revelation does not reveal Christ.

Scripture doesn't attempt to prove God's existence. It assumes that God's existence is plainly visible throughout creation to all men everywhere. It is God's revealing voice.

God's work in nature precedes God's words in history. It is a self-revelation not written, but broadly displayed in nature and history for all to see. Nature is not so much a book, but a voice. Nowhere is God's voice not heard.

Psalm 19:1-2 says *"The heavens are telling of the glory of God; and their expanse is declaring the work of His hands. Day to day pours forth speech, and night to night reveals knowledge."* Psalm 19:4 continues this thought stating *"Their line* (sound) *has gone out through all the earth, and their utterances to the end of the world."*

Note that *"telling"* and *"declaring"* are in the present tense. God is present in nature and is even now speaking.

All of nature reflects God's glory, power and otherness. Ps. 97:6 says *"The heavens declare His righteousness, and all the peoples have seen His glory."*

> *For since the creation of the world His invisible attributes, His eternal power and divine nature, have been clearly seen, being understood through what has been made, so that they are without excuse.*
> **–Romans 1:20**

God's handiwork leads us to consider our relationship with Him. Ps. 8:3-4 asks *"When I consider Your heavens, the work of Your fingers, the moon and the stars, which You have ordained, What is man that You take thought of him, and the son of man that You care for him?"*

Paul pleaded with sinners to turn to the God who created and sustained them. In Acts 14:17, Paul preached that God *"... did not leave Himself without witness, in that He did good and gave you rains from heaven and fruitful seasons, satisfying your hearts with food and gladness."*

General revelation declares the universal presence of God in the conscience of mankind. It reveals His everlasting power, deity and holiness to man's heart. Man can't deny it or excuse himself from this common witness (Ps. 14:1).

But conscience, in itself, knows no pardon and no savior. General revelation draws a man to God, but does not offer the saving knowledge of Christ. It convicts, but it can't save.

Bible verses for devotion:

Rom. 1:19-20 & 2:14-15– How does general revelation relate to conscience?

Acts 17:27–What is the purpose of general revelation?

Chapter 7

Special Revelation

Special revelation is the idea that God reveals Himself to man as the Redeemer. Special revelation communicates God's mercy and love and the way in which this forgiveness has been rendered possible.

- Special revelation is God's redemptive voice.
- Special revelation completes General revelation.
- Special revelation provides what nature and reason can't.
- Special revelation is complete in Christ.

General revelation tells us that there is a God, the Creator of all things, who is righteous and just. It tells the human conscience that it is accountable to God who is holy.

Special revelation instructs the guilty conscience that though a man merits condemnation, God will have mercy on him and offers salvation. Not only is God's mercy revealed, but also the way in which it is rendered through Jesus Christ.

Hebrews 1:1-3 says *"God, after He spoke long ago to the fathers in the prophets in many portions and in many ways, in these last days has spoken to us in His Son, whom He appointed heir of all things, through whom also He made the world. And He is the radiance of His glory and the exact representation of His nature, and upholds all things by the word of His power. When He had made purification of sins, He sat down at the right hand of the Majesty on high."*

Special revelation declares Christ as the image of the invisible God and the only way by which a relationship with God is made possible for sinners.

As the image of God, Christ is the sole and final authority in the revealing of God. 2 Cor. 1:20 says "*For as many as are the promises of God, in Him they are yes; therefore also through Him is our Amen to the glory of God through us.*" As the "*Yes*", Christ is both the realization and the reality of all God's revelation in nature, history, and Scripture. As the "*Amen*", He is the faithful and true witness. Jesus Christ is the express and concluding revelation of God.

> *For He rescued us from the domain of darkness, and transferred us to the kingdom of His beloved Son, in whom we have redemption, the forgiveness of sins. He is the image of the invisible God, the firstborn of all creation.*
> **–Colossians 1:13-15**

Before conversion, Christ as the revelation of God is external to us. He is the objective certainty of God. Upon conversion, Christ becomes the internal revelation of God to us. Christ becomes our subjective certitude of God's revelation. God's revelation becomes clearer and brighter as "*...Christ is formed in you*" (Gal. 4:19).

For our knowledge of Christ, we are dependent upon Scripture and the indwelling Spirit of Christ to illuminate our understanding of it. God has graciously chosen to fully reveal Himself to us in Christ through the Bible by His Spirit.

Bible verses for devotion:

Jn. 5:38-40, 45-47– Of who does Scripture testify?

Jn. 20:31– Why was the Bible written?

Colossians 3:16– How can the word dwell in you?

Chapter 8

Inspiration of Scripture

Inspiration is the influence of the Spirit of God upon the minds of the Scripture writers to accurately record divine revelation that is wholly trustworthy and sufficient to lead us to salvation in Jesus Christ.

- Scripture is God breathed.
- God authored the Bible through inspired men.
- God rendered Scripture to be infallible and inerrant.
- A unified witness is presented throughout the Scriptures.

In giving His revelation to the world, God has followed His ordinary method of communicating and preserving truth by means of written documents that we know as the Bible.

God inspired holy men to record His divine self-revelation. The Holy Spirit's influence was brought to bear upon the minds of the Scripture writers in order to secure putting His truth into permanent, written form.

Inspiration may often include revelation, or direct communication from God of truth which man could not attain by his unaided powers (Rev. 1:19). It may include illumination, or the quickening of man's cognitive powers to understand truth already revealed (Gal. 1:12-16). Inspiration, however, does not necessarily and always include revelation or illumination (Heb. 1:1). It is simply the divine influence which secures the transmission of needed truth to the future (Luke 1:3). But inspiration is always God's superintendence.

Since Christ, who is the divine Logos or Reason, is *"...the true Light which... enlightens every man"* (Jn. 1:9), a special influence of *"...the Spirit of Christ within them..."* (1 Pet. 1:11) rationally accounts for the fact that *"... men moved by the Holy Spirit spoke from God"* (2 Pet. 1:21).

God is perfect. As God is its source, the Bible is wholly trustworthy, the only perfect rule to guide our faith and life.

> *For this reason we also constantly thank God that when you received the word of God which you heard from us, you accepted it not as the word of men, but for what it really is, the word of God, which also performs its work in you who believe.*
> **–1 Thessalonians 2:13**

In 2 Timothy 3:16-17, Paul said *"All Scripture is inspired by God and profitable for teaching, for reproof, for correction, for training in righteousness; so that the man of God may be adequate, equipped for every good work."*

The same Holy Spirit who made the original revelation must interpret to us the record of it if we are to come to the knowledge of truth.

The testimony of the Holy Spirit combines with the teaching of the Bible to convince the earnest reader that this teaching is as a whole, and in all of its parts, beyond the power of men to communicate, and that its writing must have been put into permanent and written form by God's inspiration. So used and so interpreted, these writings are sufficient to lead us to Christ and salvation.

Bible verses for devotion:

Jn. 12:49-50–To who does Jesus ascribe His words?

Jn. 10:35– Why can't Scripture be broken?

Chapter 9

Canon of Scripture

The Canon of Scripture is the list of books of sacred Scripture recognized by believers to be the writings of men, or class of men, whose names they bear, and that they are also credible and inspired.

- We affirm the genuineness of the books of the Bible.
- We affirm the credibility of the writers of the Scriptures.
- We affirm the supernatural nature of the Bible's teaching.

Canon means a measuring reed. Therefore, it is a rule or a standard. It is the list of books regarded as true Scripture.

The determination of the Canon is not the work of the church as an organized body. We do not receive these books upon the authority of the early church Fathers or Councils. We receive them only as the Fathers and Councils received them. We receive them only by the testimony of God's Spirit. He witnesses to our hearts concerning their divine authority.

All of the books of the New Testament were not only received as genuine, but were used in more or less collected form since the latter half of the second century, with the single exception of 2 Peter. The Christian Fathers, who lived in the first half of the second century, not only quote from these books and allude to them, but testify that they were written by the apostles themselves. We are therefore compelled to refer their origin still further back, namely, to the first century, when the apostles lived.

The Bible is not simply a collection of books. The Bible is a book. It is unified in all of its revelation of God.

The Bible is made up of sixty-six books, by forty writers of all ranks. Some writers were shepherds, some were fisherman, and some were priests. Other writers were warriors, statesman, and kings. These men composed their works at intervals throughout a period of seventeen centuries.

> *You, however, continue in the things you have learned and become convinced of, knowing from whom you have learned them, and that from childhood you have known the sacred writings which are able to give you the wisdom that leads to salvation through faith which is in Christ Jesus.*
> *—2 Timothy 3:14-15*

Documents may be genuine which are written in whole or part by persons other than whose name they bear, provided these persons belonged to the same class of men. For example, the addition of Deuteronomy 34 after Moses's death does not invalidate the genuineness of the Pentateuch.

In spite of its variety of authorship and the vast separation of its writers from one another in point of time, there is a unity of subject, spirit and aim throughout the whole Bible. It is not the work of man. It is the work of God. We have no reason to doubt its authenticity or its authority.

Bible verses for devotion:

Matthew 5:17-19– What does Jesus say about the unity of spirit in the Scriptures?

Luke 24:44-47 –What does Jesus say about the unity of subject and aim in the Scriptures?

Chapter 10

Interpretation of Scripture

The Bible is in all of its parts the work of God. Each part is to be judged, not by itself alone, but in its connection with every other part. The central subject and thought which binds all parts of the Bible together, and in the light of which they are to be interpreted, is the Person and work of Jesus Christ.

- We must interpret the Scripture in context.
- We must interpret the Old Testament in light of the New.
- We must interpret the unclear in light of the clear.
- We must interpret the Scripture as it is written.
- We must not allegorize or supply meaning not written.
- We must avoid biases that effect our interpretation.
- We must be guided by God's Spirit in our interpretation.

Like ticket stubs, Scripture texts are "Not good if detached." We must put ourselves to school in every part of them. When the earlier parts are taken in connection with the later, and when each part is interpreted by the whole, difficulties of interpretation will often disappear.

We are to interpret Old Testament terms by the New Testament meaning put into them. We are to interpret the Hebrew by the Greek, not the Greek by the Hebrew. By the later usage of the New Testament, the Holy Spirit shows us what is meant by the Old Testament. Jesus often refers to the Old Testament types and symbols that pointed to Him as their true fulfillment (Mat. 12:39, 42; John 2:19; 3:14).

Taken together, with Christ as its culmination and explanation, the Bible furnishes the Christian with the only true rule of faith and practice.

Obscure passages must be interpreted in light of the plain passages. Unless the idea taught is supported by other passages, we must not ascribe divine authority to our private impressions.

> *But when He, the Spirit of truth, comes, He will guide you into all the truth; for He will not speak on His own initiative, but whatever He hears, He will speak; and He will disclose to you what is to come. He will glorify Me, for He will take of Mine and will disclose it to you.*
> **–John 16:13-14**

We must interpret Scripture in the literary sense in which each book is written. Take for example, the character of prophecy, as a rough, general sketch of the future. With its highly figurative language, and without the proper historical perspective, it is possible that we may confound the drapery with the substance, or apply its language to events to which it has no reference. We should tremble at His word (Isa. 66:2).

We must be like the Bereans who "...*received the word with great eagerness, examining the Scriptures daily to see whether these things were so*" (Acts 17:11).

The same Spirit of Christ who inspired the Bible is promised to teach us the things of Christ and lead us into all truth. Only the Holy Spirit can turn the outer word into the inner word.

Bible verses for devotion:

2 Timothy 2:15– How do we rightly divide the word?

John 14:25-26– Who is our teacher?

III. THE NATURE AND ATTRIBUTES OF GOD

Chapter 11

The Spiritual Nature of God

By describing God as spiritual, we mean that God is spiritual in substance.

- God is not a material being.
- God cannot be apprehended by any physical means.
- Without the teaching of God's Spirit, we can't know God.

God is not matter, but is spirit. He is pure spirit. Spirit is not a refined form of matter, but an immaterial substance.

Because God is spirit, He is both incorruptible and indestructible. God is not in any way dependent on matter. He is eternal and immortal. In 1 Timothy 1:17, Paul exclaims *"Now to the King eternal, immortal, invisible, the only God, be honor and glory forever and ever. Amen."*

Because God is spirit, He is invisible. In 1 Tim. 6:16, Paul praises God *"who alone possesses immortality and dwells in unapproachable light, whom no man has seen or can see. To him be honor and eternal dominion. Amen."*

1 Chr. 17:20 notes God's unique nature saying *"O Lord, there is none like You, nor is there any God besides You, according to all that we have heard with our ears."*

The passages in Scripture which seem to ascribe to God the possession of bodily parts, such as eyes and hands, are to be regarded as symbolic expressions that graciously help finite man grasp the character of the most high God.

The second commandment forbids our conceiving of God as a thing. Isaiah 40:18 asks *"To whom then will you liken God? Or what likeness will you compare with Him?"*

> *God is Spirit, and those who worship Him must worship in spirit and truth.*
> **–John 4:24**

The representation of God with body or form degrades Him to the level of the heathen gods. These representations obscure the glory of God. They misinform our idea of God, bringing it down to the low level of our own material being. To worship God in spirit and truth is to worship God as He actually is. We can only do so by His gracious self-revelation.

Because God is spirit, we can only recognize Him through spiritual means. It is divine revelation that brings us to God, not human perception or imagination.

1 Cor. 2:10-11 says *"For to us God revealed them through the Spirit; for the Spirit searches all things, even the depths of God. For who among men knows the thoughts of a man except the spirit of the man which is in him? Even so the thoughts of God no one knows except the Spirit of God."*

It is only by revelation that we can know God. The Holy Spirit reveals God to us in Jesus Christ. The longing for a tangible, incarnate God meets its satisfaction in Jesus Christ.

Bible verses for devotion:

Ex. 33:18-20; John 1:18 –Who has seen God?

Matthew 16:13-17– How did Peter apprehend who Jesus was?

Colossians 1:15 –Where do we find the image of the invisible God?

Chapter 12

The Living God

God is the living God, having in His own being the source of being and activity, both for Himself and others.

- The Scriptures represent God as the living God.
- Life implies energy, activity, and movement.
- God is not like the idols and false gods that have no life.
- Only the living God can give life and satisfaction.

Throughout Scripture, men are urged to turn *"...to God from idols to serve a living and true God"* (1 Thes. 1:9). The living God who gives us breath, watches over us, loves us, hears us, leads us and intervenes on our behalf.

If spirit in man implies life, spirit in God implies endless and inexhaustible life. The total life of the universe is only a faint image of that great energy which we call the life of God.

We do not bow down before dead idols, who cannot hear, speak, think, or move. They cannot act and can give no life.

Jer. 10:3-5 declares *"For the customs of the peoples are delusion; because it is wood cut from the forest, the work of the hands of a craftsman with a cutting tool. They decorate it with silver and with gold; they fasten it with nails and with hammers so that it will not totter. Like a scarecrow in a cucumber field are they, and they cannot speak; they must be carried, because they cannot walk! Do not fear them, for they can do no harm, nor can they do any good."*

In contrast, Jeremiah says *"But the LORD is the true God; He is the living God and the everlasting King. At His wrath the earth quakes, and the nations cannot endure His indignation. Thus you shall say to them: The gods that did not make the heavens and the earth will perish from the earth and from under the heavens"* (Jer. 10:10).

> *My soul longed and even yearned for the courts of the LORD; My heart and my flesh sing for joy to the living God.*
> **–Psalm 84:2**

King Darius was driven to say *"I make a decree that in all the dominion of my kingdom men are to fear and tremble before the God of Daniel; for He is the living God and enduring forever, and His kingdom is one which will not be destroyed, and His dominion will be forever. He delivers and rescues and performs signs and wonders in heaven and on earth, Who has also delivered Daniel from the power of the lions"* (Daniel 6:26-27).

God is not dead. God is active, engaged, and in control of all things. In Ps. 18:46, David sang *"The LORD lives! Blessed be my rock; and exalted be the God of my salvation."*

The living God, who has life in Himself, has given us His Son to be the life of the world. Christ has come *"...according to the power of an indestructible life"* (Hebrews 7:16). Because Jesus Christ lives, we have confidence that nothing can separate us from His love. Only the living God can meet all of our soul's longings.

Bible verses for devotion:

John 5:26-29 –What is meant by *"the Father has life in Himself"*?

John 14:6– What is Jesus teaching in this verse?

Chapter 13

The Personality of God

The Scriptures represent God as a personal being. This means He exercises conscious reflection and determines His actions from within.

- God is not a vague force or higher power.
- God, as a Person, is rational.
- God, as a Person, is resolute.
- God, as a Person, is relational.

God is not a force or power. God is not a philosophical or religious ideal. God is a personal being. God told Moses to tell Israel that *"I AM has sent me to you."* God is not the everlasting "IT IS" or "I WAS", but is the everlasting "I AM". "I AM" implies both personality and presence.

God is in the highest degree, self-conscious and self-determining. This means God reflects, wills and acts from within by virtue of His own free will.

Because God is a Person, He is rational. This means that God is reflective, thoughtful, and conscious of Himself and His creation. Isa. 55:8 says *"For My thoughts are not your thoughts, nor are your ways My ways, declares the LORD."*

Because God is a Person, He is resolute. This means that God is purposeful, decisive, and willful in all His actions. Job 23:13 says *"But He is unique, and who can turn Him? And what His soul desires, that He does."*

Because God is a Person, He is relational. This means that God relates to His created order. At the root of His personality is the divine capacity for affection.

God called Israel His people and set His love on them. Likewise, in the New Testament, the church is called the bride of Christ (Rev. 19:7).

God is not only *"The LORD God of your fathers, the God of Abraham, the God of Isaac, and the God of Jacob"*, but He is also the *"Savior of all men, especially of believers"* (Ex. 3:15; 1 Tim. 4:10).

> *God said to Moses, I AM WHO I AM; and He said, Thus you shall say to the sons of Israel, I AM has sent me to you. God, furthermore, said to Moses, Thus you shall say to the sons of Israel, The LORD, the God of your fathers, the God of Abraham, the God of Isaac, and the God of Jacob, has sent me to you. This is My name forever, and this is My memorial-name to all generations.*
> **–Exodus 3:14-15**

As humans, we too are persons. But we are not fully our own masters. Our personality is incomplete. Our self-determination is as limited as our self-consciousness. We reason truly, only with God's helping. We will rightly, only as God works in us to will and to do His good pleasure (Phil. 2:13). Our love only endures in His higher love (1 Jn. 4:16).

To make us truly ourselves, to be complete, we need an infinite Personality to supplement and energize our own.

Bible verses for devotion:

Deuteronomy 7:6-8 –How does God relate to us?

Colossians 2:9-10– How is our person completed?

Chapter 14

The Triunity of God

The doctrine of the Trinity is only a designation of four facts: (1) the Father is God; (2) the Son is God; (3) the Spirit is God; (4) there is but one God.

- The Father, the Son and the Spirit are each God.
- Scripture represents them as distinct Persons.
- While there are three Persons, there is but one essence.
- The three Persons aren't due to mere roles or phases.
- The three Persons are eternally inherent in God's nature.
- The three Persons, Father, Son and Holy Spirit are equal.
- The Trinity is inscrutable, but it is not self-contradictory.

The term "Trinity" is not found in Scripture, although the conception it expresses is Scriptural. The doctrine of the Trinity teaches that there are three eternal distinctions in the substance of God. Or conversely, there is one God with three distinctions in His being.

The Father, Son, and Holy Spirit each possess one and the same divine nature, though in a different manner.

The idea of the Trinity does not teach that there are three Gods united in one or acting in unison. The Trinity is not a mere partnership in which each member can sign the name of the firm. That is a unity of council and operation only, not of essence. Nor does the idea of the Trinity teach that God merely manifests Himself in three different ways or roles. That would be an appearance of unity with no substance.

The undivided essence of the Godhead belongs equally to each of the Persons. The Father, Son, and Holy Spirit are each equally God. Each Person possesses all the substance and all the attributes of Diety. Neither Person is God without the others. Each Person, with the others, is God. There is one essence.

> *After being baptized, Jesus came up immediately from the water; and behold, the heavens were opened, and He saw the Spirit of God descending as a dove and lighting on Him, and behold, a voice out of the heavens said, This is My beloved Son, in whom I am well-pleased.*
> **–Matthew 3:16-17**

Scripture alludes to the eternal generation of the Son and the proceeding of the Spirit from both the Father and the Son. These terms do not represent inequality. Rather, the Father, Son, and Holy Spirit are equal in essence and glory.

These terms refer to an order of personality, office, and operation in which the Father works through the Son, and both the Father and the Son through the Spirit. This order is perfectly consistent with equality. Priority is not necessarily superiority. Each is the equal and proper object of worship.

The precise manner of God's triune existence is unrevealed to us and is beyond our comprehension. But we do grasp the four basic facts of the Trinity. The doctrine of the Trinity is foundational to a proper understanding of God's revelation and redemption (Hebrews 9:14). In Jesus Christ, God is revealed and human nature is lifted up into the life and communion of the eternal Trinity.

> *Bible verses for devotion:*
>
> **Gal. 4:4-6**– How are we united into the life of God?

Chapter 15

The Infinity of God

The infinity of God means that the divine nature has no limits or bounds. God is in no way limited by the universe. God is unlimited in resource, without end and beyond our ability to comprehend.

- God alone is infinite.
- God has infinite energy of spiritual life.
- God is unexhausted by His present activities.
- God's infinity colors our understanding of His attributes.
- The infinite God condescends to finite man for us to live.

God alone is infinite. The universe and all that is within it is finite, limited and dependent on Him.

God is never wholly absorbed by what He is doing or capable of doing nothing more. God's life operates unspent. There is ever more to follow. God's reserves are infinite.

The attribute of infinity qualifies all His other attributes, for God is infinite in all His nature. God's infinity is therefore foundational for representations of His majesty and glory.

Psalm 147:4-5 says *"He counts the number of the stars; He gives names to all of them. Great is our Lord and abundant in strength; His understanding is infinite."*

There is transcendence in God which no self-revelation exhausts, whether in creation or redemption, law or promise. God's works and ways can't fully express His infinite glory.

Transcendence is not mere outsideness. It is rather boundless supply from within.

Infinity implies that God exists in no necessary relation to finite things or beings, and that whatever limitation of the divine nature results from their existence is, on the part of God, a self-limitation. This is God's gracious condescension to man.

> *Do you not know? Have you not heard? The Everlasting God, the LORD, the Creator of the ends of the earth, does not become weary or tired. His understanding is inscrutable. He gives strength to the weary, and to him who lacks might He increases power.*
> *–Isaiah 40:28-29*

Psalm 113:5-8 asks *"Who is like the LORD our God, Who is enthroned on high, Who humbles Himself to behold the things that are in heaven and in the earth? He raises the poor from the dust and lifts the needy from the ash heap, to make them sit with princes, with the princes of His people."* God makes Himself little so He can make us great.

It is amazing that the infinite God, who is so great and high above us, is also a God who is near to us. In Immanuel, we find that He is truly *"God with us"* (Mat. 1:23).

Because God is infinite, He can love each believer as much as if that single soul was the only one for whom He had to care for. In all things, the whole heart of God is engaged and busy with plans for the good of every Christian.

Bible verses for devotion:

Phil. 4:19-20– Do you trust the infinite God with your finite needs?

Rom. 11:33-36– Where does God's infinity lead us?

Chapter 16

The Self-Existence of God

> *The self-existence of God means that God has the ground of His existence in Himself.*

- God is the uncaused Being.
- God has no beginning.
- God's existence is contingent on nothing.
- God is the living spring of all energy and of all being.

The Bible begins with *"In the beginning God...."* God was already there. God has no beginning. He has always been.

God revealed His name to Israel through Moses. Exodus 6:2-3 records *"God spoke further to Moses and said to him, I am the LORD; and I appeared to Abraham, to Isaac, and Jacob, as God Almighty, but by My name, LORD, I did not make Myself known to them."* The name, LORD, means "I AM". God's very name signifies that it is His nature to be.

God has not a cause or beginning, rather He is the beginning and cause of all living things. God is not created, but He is the Creator of all things. In Isaiah 43:13, God reminds us *"Even from eternity I am He..."*

In Revelation 1:8, Jesus says *"I am the Alpha and the Omega, says the Lord God, who is and who was and who is to come, the Almighty."* Likewise, in Colossians 1:17, Paul wrote *"He is before all things, and in Him all things hold together."* Here we see with clarity that Christ is self-existent and apart from Him, nothing can exist.

The apostle Paul reasoned with the men of Athens, declaring to them that God is the very ground of being.

In Acts 17:24-28, Paul says *"The God who made the world and all things in it, since He is Lord of heaven and earth, does not dwell in temples made with hands; nor is He served by human hands, as though He needed anything, since He Himself gives to all people life and breath and all things; and He made from one man every nation of mankind to live on all the face of the earth, having determined their appointed times and the boundaries of their habitation, that they would seek God, if perhaps they might grope for Him and find Him, though He is not far from each one of us; for in Him we live and move and exist, as even some of your own poets have said, For we also are His children."*

> *Lord, You have been our dwelling place in all generations. Before the mountains were born or You gave birth to the earth and the world, even from everlasting to everlasting, You are God.*
> **–Psalm 90:1-2**

Everything we come into contact with in our world has its source of existence outside of itself. But God is not thus dependent. He needs nothing outside Himself to exist.

Self-existence is certainly incomprehensible to us, yet it is God's nature. The existence of God is not a contingent, but a necessary existence. All things are dependent on God.

Bible verses for devotion:

Psalm 93:2–How long has God been on His throne?

Acts 17:24-28– Does God need anything?

Chapter 17

The Immutability of God

The nature, attributes, and will of God are exempt from all change.

- God is absolute perfection.
- No change to better or worse is possible with God.
- No cause for such change exists in God or from without.
- Immutability is consistent with constant activity.
- Immutability is consistent with perfect freedom.

Immutability teaches that God is constant and consistent in His Person, will, and actions. In God there is no fickleness.

God cannot increase or decrease, progress or deteriorate, contract or develop. Malachi 3:6 says *"For I, the LORD, do not change..."*

All change must be to better or to worse. Because God is absolute perfection, no change is possible that would make Him better. Likewise, change to the worse would be equally impossible and inconsistent with His infinite perfection.

James 1:17 says *"Every good thing given and every perfect gift is from above, coming down from the Father of lights, with whom there is no variation or shifting shadow."*

Immutability must not be confused with immobility. Scripture reveals a God who is active, engaged and at work in the universe He created. God as unchanging is perfectly consistent with His constant activity in nature and in grace.

Scripture sometimes speaks of God changing His mind or ways. This is simply a way of relating God's unchanging character to a change in man toward God.

For example, Genesis 6:6 says *"The LORD was sorry that He had made man on the earth, and He was grieved in His heart."* This should be interpreted in light of Numbers 23:19 *"God is not a man, that He should lie, nor a son of man, that He should repent. Has He said, and will He not do it? Or has He spoken, and will He not make it good?"*

> *Of old You founded the earth, and the heavens are the work of Your hands. Even they will perish, but You endure; and all of them will wear out like a garment; like clothing You will change them and they will be changed. But You are the same, and Your years will not come to an end.*
> **–Psalm 102:25-27**

God's unchanging holiness requires Him to treat the wicked differently from the righteous. When the righteous become wicked, His treatment of them must change.

When we change, God responds in a way consistent with His character. The sun is not fickle because it melts the wax but hardens the clay. The change is not in the sun, but in the objects it shines on. There is no varying in God. *"Jesus Christ is the same yesterday, today, and forever"* (Heb. 13:8).

Bible verses for devotion:

1 Samuel 15:11, 29– Do these verses show a change in God or in man?

Malachi 3:6-7– How is God's immutability a consolation to the faithful, but a terror to God's enemies?

Chapter 18

The Eternity of God

God's nature is without beginning or end. He is free from all succession of time. He is the cause of time.

- God's nature is not subject to the law of time.
- God is not in time.
- Time is God's gift to us.

God gave both the world and time their existence.

Time is a relation of a finite existence. All finite creatures have a linear existence beginning at their creation.

As finite beings, we experience life as a sequence of events. We have a past, a present and a future. This frames our knowledge and experience in this world.

Our God is infinite. He has no beginning and He has no end. He alone is eternal. Eternity is infinity in its relation to time. God is king always and forever!

God is conscious not, in time, but of time and all that infinite time contains. God stands apart from time.

2 Peter 3:8 says *"But do not let this one fact escape your notice, beloved, that with the Lord one day is like a thousand years, and a thousand years like one day."*

God experiences the whole symphony of life at once. God unites in timeless perception the whole succession of finite events. The infinite God has infinite or eternal vision.

To God, past, present and future are one eternal "now".

> *I am the Alpha and the Omega, says the LORD, who is and who was and who is to come, the Almighty.*
> **–Revelation 1:8**

This does not mean that the eternal God, who instituted time at creation, sees no distinction between past, present and future.

What this means is that God sees the past and the future as vividly as He sees the present.

This helps us grasp the patience, the long-suffering, and the expectation of God. Ps. 86:15 proclaims *"But You, O Lord, are a God merciful and gracious, slow to anger and abundant in lovingkindness and truth."*

Likewise, 2 Peter 3:9 sates *"The Lord is not slow about His promise, as some count slowness, but is patient toward you, not wishing for any to perish but for all to come to repentance."*

God, in His grace and wisdom, allows us to experience time in successive moments, not simultaneously, thus preventing infinite confusion. Ps. 103:14 tells us that God *"...knows our frame; He is mindful that we are but dust."*

God created time to provide us perspective regarding our past, to order our present, and to give us hope for our future.

Let us pray like Moses prayed in Psalm 90:12, *"So teach us to number our days, that we may present to You a heart of wisdom."*

Bible verses for devotion:

Psalm 103:15-17 –How is our nature contrasted with God's nature?

Rev. 1:17– Does God's eternity encourage you?

Chapter 19

The Immensity of God

God's nature has no limitations of space. As God is spirit, He cannot be contained or limited by space. God transcends space. Yet His presence fills all space.

- God cannot be contained by His creation.
- God is fully present everywhere in space.

God is infinite. He can't be contained. He has no limits or bounds. As God is spiritual in His nature, He is beyond all spatial limitations.

God is therefore immense. Immensity is infinity in its relation to space. God transcends all things.

In Acts 7:47-48, Stephen said *"But Solomon built Him a house. However, the Most High does not dwell in temples made with hands..."* Here, Stephen is declaring that God can't be confined to one place.

In Acts 7:49-50, Stephen references Isaiah saying *"Heaven is My throne, and earth is the footstool of My feet. What kind of house will you build for Me? says the Lord, or what place is there for My repose? Was it not My hand which made all these things?"* Here, Stephen is teaching that God is over and above the world, and all that He has created.

God not only occupies all space, but He occupies all spaces fully. God's immensity means that He fills every part of space with His whole Person. God is king everywhere.

Immensity highlights God's transcendence. God not only occupies all space, but He is beyond all space. He is both transcendent as well as immanent. God is rather unspatial, even while He remains the Lord of space.

> *But will God indeed dwell on the earth? Behold, heaven and the highest heaven cannot contain You, how much less this house which I have built!*
> **–1 Kings 8:27**

God gave both the world and space their existence. Space is a relation of a finite existence. All created beings have a confined existence, occupying a limited space.

As finite beings, we experience life within the confines of space. We can only occupy one space at a time. We cannot be both here and there at the same time. This frames our limited existence and experience in this world.

It is hard for us to comprehend that God is completely present in all places throughout the universe, while at the same time He is beyond space itself. Yet it is a great comfort.

Isaiah 40:12 asks *"Who has measured the waters in the hollow of His hand, and marked off the heavens by the span, and weighed the mountains in a balance and the hills in a pair of scales?"*

Isaiah 40:22 answers *"It is He who sits above the circle of the earth, and its inhabitants are like grasshoppers, who stretches out the heavens like a curtain, and spreads them out like a tent to dwell in."* God's infinite immensity is truly glorious!

Bible verses for devotion:

Psalm 8:1–Does God's immensity amaze you?

Isaiah 66:1-2– Does immensity preclude nearness?

Chapter 20

The Omnipresence of God

God, in the totality of His essence, fully penetrates and fills the universe in all of its parts.

- There is not a place where God is not completely present.
- God is fully present with His whole being.
- God is always undivided in attention and wholly engaged.

Because God is infinitely immense, He is omnipresent. This means that God is everywhere present at all times.

God's immensity highlights His transcendence, or His being above and beyond creation. God's omnipresence highlights God's immanence or His nearness to creation.

The one essence of God is present at the same moment in all places. He is here and there simultaneously. If God is not truly everywhere, He could not be truly God anywhere.

Because God fills all of heaven and earth with His presence, He is always near to us in every place. Paul said that *"...He is not far from each one of us"* (Acts 17:27).

Our ever present God is also fully present everywhere. God must be present in all His essence and all His attributes in all places. God can't leave His holiness behind. God can't fail to uphold justice. God can't cease to show His love and care. God is not like Baal, whose prophets cried aloud and cut themselves, *"...but there was no voice, no one answered, and no one paid attention"* (1 Kings 18:29).

In Jeremiah 23:23-24, God asks us *"Am I a God who is near, declares the LORD, and not a God far off? Can a man hide himself in hiding places so I do not see him? declares the LORD; Do I not fill the heavens and the earth? declares the LORD."*

Our reliance on God and our very communion with Him is grounded in His omnipresence. In every individual heart and in every individual church, there abides the whole of Christ. In Romans 8:39, Paul confidently asserts that nothing *"...will be able to separate us from the love of God, which is in Christ Jesus our Lord."*

> *Where can I go from Your Spirit? Or where can I flee from Your presence? If I ascend to heaven, You are there; If I make my bed in Sheol, behold, You are there. If I take the wings of the dawn, if I dwell in the remotest part of the sea, even there Your hand will lead me, and Your right hand will lay hold of me. If I say, Surely the darkness will overwhelm me, and the light around me will be night, even the darkness is not dark to You, and the night is as bright as the day. Darkness and light are alike to You.*
> **–Psalm 139:7-12**

God's omnipresence assures us that He is always present with us. Indeed He is fully present with us. Our communion with God is sweet as He is in every heart and in the ends of the earth to answer prayer. Psalm 121:5 says *"The LORD is your keeper; The LORD is your shade on your right hand."*

Bible verses for devotion:

Isaiah 57:15– Where does God dwell?

Matthew 28:20– When is Jesus with us?

Chapter 21

The Omniscience of God

God is all knowing. Omniscience is God's perfect and eternal knowledge of all things, whether they are actual or possible, past, present, or future. God's knowledge is:

- True- Perfectly corresponding to the reality of things.
- Distinct- Complete and free of vagueness or confusion.
- Immediate- Not obtained through sense or imagination.
- Simultaneous- Unacquired by observations or reasoning.
- Eternal- Comprehended in one timeless act of God.

God's knowledge of all things is absolutely perfect. God's knowledge is perfect based in His infinity. God's knowledge is complete. There is nothing unclear or unknown to Him.

In God's perfect knowledge, there is no growth, reflection or reasoning. If His knowledge could be expanded or improved, His wisdom would not be infinite or perfect.

God's knowledge is eternal. He has known all things from before the foundations of the world. Hence, there is no discovery or surprise with God. His knowledge wasn't obtained through successive observations. Rather, God's knowledge is always immediate, direct and complete.

Isa. 40:13-14 asks *"Who has directed the Spirit of the Lord, or as His counselor has informed Him? Whom did He consult, and who gave Him understanding? Who taught Him in the path of justice and taught Him knowledge, and informed Him of the way of understanding?"*

[handwritten: you were created uniquely and for a purpose. God knows everything about you because he created you. And he loves you. He knows even the number of hairs on your head!]

God knows the stars (Ps. 147:4), and the sparrows (Mat. 10:29). He knows our works (Ps. 33:13-15), our hearts and thoughts (Acts 15:8, Ps. 139:2), our wants (Mat. 6:8), even the number of hairs on our head (Mat. 10:30). God perfectly knows the past (Mal. 3:16). He knows what is ideally possible (Mat. 11:23). He knows for certain what will be (Isa. 46:9-10, Isa. 53, Rev. 13:8).

> *O LORD, You have searched me and known me. You know when I sit down and when I rise up; You understand my thought from afar. You scrutinize my path and my lying down, and are intimately acquainted with all my ways. Even before there is a word on my tongue, behold, O LORD, You know it altogether.*
> *—Psalm 139:1-4*

Hebrews 4:13 says *"And there is no creature hidden from His sight, but all things are open and laid bare to the eyes of Him with whom we must give account."* His omniscience is frightening to the wicked, but comforting to believers. We can never truthfully say *"My way is hidden from the LORD"* (Isa. 40:27).

Psalm 40:5 comforts us by declaring *"...Your thoughts toward us...would be too numerous to count."* This is not because there is succession in God's knowledge, alternating between remembering and forgetting. God's thoughts can't be counted because there is never a moment of our existence in which we are out of His mind. He is always thinking of us.

Bible verses for devotion:

Acts 15:18 –When did God's knowledge begin?

Psalm 147:5– Is God's knowledge limited?

Chapter 22

The Omnipotence of God

God is all powerful over all things. God does all that He wills. His power is never exhausted.

- God is almighty in all His works.
- God's power is only limited by His will and nature.
- God's power is the ground of our trust and fear.

Ps. 135:5-6 proclaims that *"...the Lord is great and that our Lord is above all gods. Whatever the Lord pleases, He does, in heaven and in earth, in the seas and in all deeps."*

Throughout the Scriptures, we see God exercising His power over the universe and the lives of all His creatures. He has no equal.

God not only has absolute power over all creation, but He has the ability to perform whatever He wills. Job 23:13 says *"But He is unique, and who can turn Him? And what His soul desires, that He does."*

In Genesis 18:14, God asks Abraham *"Is anything too difficult for the Lord?"* In Matthew 19:26, Jesus taught His disciples that *"...with God all things are possible."*

Because God is infinite, His power is inexhaustible. When dynamite goes off, it all goes off; there is no reserve. This is not so with God. God uses as much of His power as He pleases. His reserves are infinite. His power is unspent. He *"...is able to do far more abundantly..."* (Eph. 3:20).

God has no external limitations. There is nothing outside of God that can confine or limit Him in any manner.

> *Even from eternity I am He, and there is none who can deliver out of My hand; I act and who can reverse it?*
> **–Isaiah 43:13**

God's power is only self-limited. His power is limited by both His nature and will.

God can't do things that are contrary to His nature. God's nature doesn't change. For example, God can't lie, sin, or die. To do such things would not imply power, but impotence.

God's power is also self-limited by His wise and holy will. For example, God humbled Himself to the taking of human flesh in the Person of Jesus Christ.

Even human freedom is not rendered impossible by divine omnipotence, but exists by virtue of it. God can do all things, but in His self-limitation, He does not do all things.

This self-limitation is actually an act of His omnipotence. His self-limitation is free, proceeding from neither external nor internal compulsion. God's self-limitation is the act and manifestation of His power. God has power over His power.

God's omnipotence is the ground of trust, as well as of fear, on the part of God's creatures. It is awe inspiring.

We share in the wonder that Job expressed in Job 26:14, *"Behold, these are the fringes of His ways; and how faint a word we hear of Him! But His mighty thunder, who can understand?"*

Bible verses for devotion:

Job 42:2, John 10:29– Do you share this confidence?

Philippians 2:5-8–How is this omnipotence?

Chapter 23

The Truthfulness of God

God is truth and the source of truth. God is truth in His very being and expression.

- Truth is God perfectly revealed and known.
- Because God is true, His revelation is always trustworthy.
- Because God is true, He faithfully fulfills His promises.

God is truth in His very being. God is eternally true, apart from and before all creation.

Deuteronomy 32:4 says *"The Rock! His work is perfect, for all His ways are just; A God of faithfulness and without injustice, righteous and upright is He."*

Truth is not arbitrary, — it is matter of being — the being of God. As God is infinite, He is infinitely true in His whole being. God knows and wills truth because He is truth. His will does not make truth, but truth rather makes God's will.

If God can make truth to be falsehood, and injustice to be justice, then God is indifferent to truth or falsehood, to good or evil, and He ceases thereby to be God. To make truth and good matters of mere will, instead of regarding them as characteristics of God's being, is to deny that anything is true or good in itself.

All truth among men, whether mathematical, logical, moral, or religious, is to be regarded as having its foundation in God's nature and as disclosing facts in the being of God.

The one unifying current which these truths partially reveal is the outgoing work of Christ, the divine Word.

Christ is the one and only revealer of God. Because Christ is the truth of God, we succeed in our search for truth only as we recognize Him.

> *Jesus said to him, I am the way, and the truth, and the life; no one comes to the Father but through Me.*
> **–John 14:6**

We learn truth due to the teaching role of the Holy Spirit. In John 14:17, Jesus described the Holy Spirit as *"the Spirit of truth"*. The doctrine of the Trinity is therefore the necessary complement to the doctrine of God's truth.

God is true not only in His being, but in His revelation. In God, the outer expression and the inward reality always correspond. God's truth guarantees His revelation is true. God's revelation will never be contradicted, but will rather prove to have in it more truth than we ever dreamed.

Psalm 119:160 teaches us that *"The sum of Your word is truth, and every one of Your righteous ordinances is everlasting."*

Furthermore, God's truth assures us of His faithfulness to perform all that He has promised. 2 Tim. 2:13 says *"If we are faithless, He remains faithful, for He cannot deny Himself."*

Because God is forever true, so are His promises. Psalm 91:4 says *"...His faithfulness is a shield and bulwark."*

Bible verses for devotion:

1 John 5:20– Do you share in God's truth?

Psalm 119:162– What is your treasure?

Chapter 24

The Love of God

Love is God's desire to impart Himself, to fill and bless the other person with Himself, and to possess them for His own union and fellowship.

- The object of God's eternal love can only be Himself.
- God is the only adequate object of His perfect love.
- God loves humanity for His sake.
- God's love is the giving of Himself.
- God's love manifests His perfection and works in man.

The only sufficient object of God's love is the image of His own perfections, for that alone is equal to Himself.

The eternal and perfect object of God's love is His own nature. Psalm 145:3 declares *"Great is the Lord, and highly to be praised, and His greatness is unsearchable."*

Love precedes creation and is the ground of creation. The universe did not pre-exist. Finite creation could never be a proper object of love for the infinite God. Psalm 95:6 says *"Come, let us worship and bow down, let us kneel before the Lord our Maker."*

The love of God can't find perfect satisfaction outside His own holiness and infinite perfections (Phil. 2:9-11). In His Tri-unity, God has perfect self-impartation, union and fellowship. Rom. 9:5 states that God is *"...blessed forever."* As Trinity, God's love finds its perfect object. The love of God is to be understood only in the light of the Trinity.

God's love toward us is His desire to give Himself to us, to penetrate us with Him, and thereby bring us into His union and spiritual fellowship.

> *We have come to know and have believed the love which God has for us. God is love, and the one who abides in love abides in God, and God abides in him.*
> *−1 John 4:16*

God's love for us includes His mercy and goodness to all men (Ps. 145:8-9). God's mercy leads Him to seek the earthly good and eternal salvation of those who have opposed themselves to His will, even at the cost of infinite self-sacrifice. Despite our sin, God still sees His image in us.

Eph. 2:4-5 exalts His mercy, saying *"But God, being rich in mercy, because of His great love with which He loved us, even when we were dead in our transgressions, made us alive together with Christ (by grace you have been saved)."*

God's goodness leads Him to communicate of His own life and blessedness to those who are His own. It is a special love reserved for His children, united to Him in Christ.

Ephesians 2:6-7 illustrates the goodness of God who *"... raised us up with Him, and seated us with Him in the heavenly places in Christ Jesus, so that in the ages to come He might show the surpassing riches of His grace in kindness toward us in Christ Jesus."*

God imparts Himself to us in Christ, filling and blessing us by His Spirit, and possessing us in union and fellowship.

Bible verses for devotion:

Psalm 17:15–How does God love Himself in us?

Romans 5:8– How are love and giving related?

Chapter 25

The Holiness of God

Holiness is God's declaration and willing of His own infinite moral perfection and purity.

- God is the source and standard of right.
- God is not only holy in His nature, but in all His works.
- Holiness is God's self-affirmation and self-willing.
- Holiness asserts God as our highest motive and chief end.

Holiness is the fundamental attribute in God. Holiness implies purity (Heb. 12:29) and transcendence (Ps. 47:8). Throughout Scripture, God constantly asserts His holiness. Even in heaven, where there is no sin, there is the same reiteration: *"Holy, holy, holy is the LORD of hosts"* (Isa. 6:3); *"Holy, holy, holy is the LORD God, the Almighty"* (Rev. 4:8).

God is both infinitely pure and infinitely above us in His glory. 1 Jn. 1:5 tells us that *"...God is Light, and in Him there is no darkness at all."* This teaches us that God is separate and free from all stain and wrong. It also teaches us that He is perfect purity revealed, different from all others, producing joy and life. Ps. 96:9 says *"Oh, worship the LORD in holy attire; Tremble before Him, all the earth."*

Because God is holy, His will and all His works are holy. God cannot deny Himself because He is fundamentally holy. As God alone is wholly holy, His self-affirmation is unfailing. The first petition of our Lord's Prayer in Mat. 6:9-10 is not *"Your kingdom come"*, but it is *"Hallowed be Your name"*.

God is not under law, nor above law. He is law. God is subject to no law but the law of His own nature. God is the one source and author of law.

> *Thus you are to be holy to Me, for I the LORD am holy, and I have set you apart from the peoples to be Mine.*
> –Leviticus 20:26

The whole momentum of God's being is behind moral law. That law is His self-expression. His benevolent yet fearsome arm is ever defending and enforcing it. God must maintain His holiness, for this is His very Godhead.

God exercises His holiness toward us in righteousness and justice. His righteousness requires our conformity to the moral perfection of God. God's justice visits non-conformity to His perfection with penalty. In righteousness, God reveals His love of holiness. In justice, God reveals His hatred of sin. Psalm 97:2 declares that "...*Righteousness and justice are the foundation of His throne.*" This is God's self-affirmation.

In 1 Peter 1:16, God's commands us to "*Be holy*", where the ground of obligation assigned is simply and only: "*for I am holy.*" Jesus instructed us in Mat. 5:48 "*Therefore you are to be perfect*", where the standard laid down is: "*as your heavenly Father is perfect.*" This is God's self-willing.

In God, we have the ground of all moral obligation. He is infinite purity. Holiness, since it is God's self-affirmation and self-willing, furnishes the guarantee that God's love will not fail to secure its end, and that all things will serve His purpose. Romans 11:36 assures us of this by proclaiming "*For from Him, and through Him, and to Him are all things. To Him be the glory forever. Amen.*"

Bible verse for devotion:

Isaiah 5:16–How is God exalted and hallowed?

IV. THE DECREES AND WORKS OF GOD

Chapter 26

The Decrees of God

The decrees of God refer to God's eternal plan by which God has rendered certain all the events of the universe, past, present and future.

- The decrees seem many; in reality they are but one plan.
- The decrees are an eternal act of an infinitely perfect will.
- The decrees don't compel or obligate the will of man.
- All human acts, evil or good, are objects of God's decree.
- In regard to evil, God's decrees are only permissive.

The Scriptures declare that all things are included in God's plan. For example, God decrees the stability of the physical universe (Ps. 119:89-91); the circumstances of nations (Acts 17:26); the length of human life (Job 14:5); the mode of our death (John 21:19); even the free acts of men, both good acts and evil acts (Eph. 2:10, Gen. 50:20, Acts 2:23, Acts 4:27-28, Rev. 17:17). Scripture teaches that God has decreed the salvation of believers (Eph. 1:4-5, 11); the establishment of Christ's kingdom (Ps. 2:7-8); and the work of Christ and of His people in establishing it (Eph. 3:10-11).

God's decrees are certain from eternity. God's foreknowledge is not of possible events, but of what is certain to be. The certainty of future events which God foreknew could have had its ground only in His decree, since He alone existed to be the ground and explanation of this certainty.

God's decrees are framed by His wisdom and goodness.

God's plan vs. free will

God's plan does not conflict with man's free will. Because Scripture assures us that free agency exists, it must exist by God's decree. Though we may be ignorant of the method in which the decrees are executed, we have no right to doubt either the decrees or the freedom. God's decrees are not addressed to men, do not force human action, and become known only after the event. All conflict between God's sovereign will and man's free will must therefore be only apparent and not real.

> *Remember the former things long past, for I am God, and there is no other; I am God, and there is no one like Me, declaring the end from the beginning, and from ancient times things which have not been done, saying, My purpose will be established, and I will accomplish all My good pleasure.*
> *–Isaiah 46:9-10*

In regard to sin, God decrees to permit it but not to directly produce it. God creates and preserves human wills which, in their own self-chosen courses, will be and do evil. God's decrees do not make Him the author of sin, but the author of free beings who are themselves the authors of sin. Sin was permitted because it could be overruled and without it, God's justice and God's mercy alike would be unrevealed.

God's plan inspires humility and awe of His unsearchable counsels and absolute sovereignty. It gives us confidence that God has wisely ordered the minutest of details to make all things work for the good of His people and the triumph of His kingdom. It shows God's enemies that their sins have been foreseen and provided for in God's plan, if they repent.

Bible verse for devotion:

Romans 8:28– How does this strengthen your faith?

"And we know that in all things God works for the good of those who love him, who have been called according to his purpose." - Romans 8:28

Chapter 27

Creation

Creation is the free act of the triune God by which in the beginning He made all things out of nothing for His own glory.

- Creation is not a fashioning of pre-existing materials.
- Creation is making that to exist which once did not exist.
- All the Persons of the Trinity have a part in creation.
- God's supreme end in creation is His own glory.

The Bible begins with *"In the beginning, God created the heavens and the earth"* (Gen. 1:1).

In the beginning, there was God and nothing else. God created the world out of nothing, in other words, with no pre-existing materials. Hebrews 11:3 says *"By faith we understand that the worlds were prepared by the word of God, so that what is seen was not made out of things which are visible."* Nothing exists apart from God's creative action.

God spoke the universe into existence. Psalm 33:6, 9 tells us *"By the word of the LORD the heavens were made, and by the breath of His mouth all their host...For He spoke, and it was done; He commanded, and it stood fast."*

God alone created the universe and all that is in it. Isaiah 44:24 proclaims *"Thus says the LORD, your Redeemer, and the one who formed you from the womb: I the LORD, am the maker of all things, stretching out the heavens by Myself and spreading out the earth all alone."*

Creation is the work of each Person of the Godhead. Scripture presents the Father as the originating cause, the Son as the mediating cause, and the Spirit as the realizing cause of creation.

John 1:3 teaches the Son's role in creation saying *"All things came into being through Him, and apart from Him nothing came into being that has come into being."*

> *Lift up your eyes on high, and see who has created these stars, the One who leads forth their host by number, He calls them all by name; because of the greatness of His might and the strength of His power, not one of them is missing.*
> –Isaiah 40:26

In Genesis 1:2, we read that the Holy Spirit was brooding over the face of the waters, as an eagle flutters over her nest. In Job 33:4, Job states *"The Spirit of God has made me, and the breath of the Almighty gives me life."*

God's chief end in creation is nothing outside Himself, but only His own glory. The glory of the infinitely perfect God is revealed in and through His creation. By expressing Himself in His creation, God communicates to His creatures the utmost possible good. In His revelation, we are shown that our interests are bound up in His (Ps. 100).

Col. 1:16-17 says *"For by Him all things were created, both in the heavens and on earth, visible and invisible, whether thrones or dominions or rulers or authorities—all things have been created through Him and for Him. He is before all things, and in Him all things hold together."*

Bible verses for devotion:

Genesis 1 & 2–Read and meditate on these chapters.

Chapter 28

Preservation

Preservation is the continuous operation of God by which He maintains in existence all the things He has created, together with the properties and powers with which He has endowed them.

- Preservation is not a mere refraining to destroy.
- Preservation is a continuous willing to sustain all things.
- No person or force can exist or act without preservation.
- Preservation teaches us that all things depend on God.

Preservation is God's continuous willing. All natural forces and all personal beings bear testimony to the will of God which originated them and continually sustains them.

The physical universe is in no sense independent of God. Its forces are only the constant willing of God, and its laws are only the habits of God.

Hebrews 1:3 states that Christ "...*upholds all things by the word of His power.*" Psalm 36:6 says "...*O LORD, You preserve man and beast.*"

Psalm 104:27-30 declares "*They all wait for You to give them their food in due season. You give to them, they gather it up; You open Your hand, they are satisfied with good. You hide Your face, they are dismayed; You take away their spirit, they expire and return to their dust. You send forth Your Spirit, they are created; and You renew the face of the ground.*"

The apostle Paul boldly preached in Acts 17:28 *"for in Him we live and move and exist..."*

God's upholding of our existence does not destroy or absorb our own being or the powers we have been given.

Humans are upheld by God's will, but human wills do not always obey the divine will. They may even oppose it.

Man's free will exists only by God's self-limitation. However, the being that sins can maintain its existence only through the preserving agency of God.

> *You alone are the Lord. You have made the heavens, the heaven of heavens with all their host, the earth and all that is on it, the seas and all that is in them. You give life to all of them and the heavenly host bows down before You.*
> **–Nehemiah 9:6**

These are indeed upheld by God in their being, but opposed by God in their conduct. Preservation leaves room for human freedom, responsibility, sin, and guilt.

In God's inexhaustible fullness of life there are no burdens involved in the upholding of the universe that He has created. God's infinity turns into sources of delight all that would seem burdensome to man.

God's work of preservation displays the same glory, perfection, majesty, and unity as does His work of creation.

God has promised us that *"While the earth remains, seedtime and harvest, and cold and heat, and summer and winter, and day and night shall not cease* (Genesis 8:22).

Bible verses for devotion:

Ps. 66:8-9–How do we respond to His preservation?

Chapter 29

Providence

Providence is the continuous operation of God by which He makes all the events of the physical and moral universe fulfill His purpose.

- Providence is not mere foresight.
- Providence is the directing of all the events of history.

Creation explains the existence of the universe. Preservation explains its continuance. Providence explains its development and progress.

Just as the plan of God is all-comprehending, likewise providence, which executes the plan, is all-comprehending. Providence embraces within its scope things small and great, and exercises care over individuals as well as over classes.

In respect to the good acts of men, providence embraces all those natural influences of birth and surroundings which prepare men for the operation of God's word and Spirit, and which constitute motives to obedience.

Paul acknowledged God's providence in Gal. 1:15-16, testifying "*...God, who had set me apart even from my mother's womb and called me through His grace, was pleased to reveal His Son in me so that I might preach...*"

In respect to the evil acts of men, providence is never described as the producing cause of sin, but is by turns preventive, permissive, directive, and determinative.

Preventative providence is found in Genesis 20:6 where God told Abimelech *"...I also kept you from sinning against Me; therefore I did not let you touch her."*

Permissive providence is typified in Romans 1:28 which says *"And just as they did not see fit to acknowledge God any longer, God gave them over to a depraved mind, to do those things which are not proper."*

Directive providence is evidenced in Genesis 50:20 when Joseph tells his brothers *"As for you, you meant evil against me, but God meant it for good in order to bring about this present result, to preserve many people alive."*

> *For His dominion is an everlasting dominion, and His kingdom endures from generation to generation. All the inhabitants of the earth are accounted as nothing, but He does according to His will in the host of heaven and among the inhabitants of the earth; and no one can ward off His hand or say to Him, 'What have You done'?*
> *—Daniel 4:34-35*

Determinative providence is found in Job 1:12 which says *"Then the LORD said to Satan, Behold, all that he has is in your power, only do not put forth your hand on him."*

God's providence is grasped only when we consider that Christ is the revealer of God, and that His suffering for sin opens to us the heart of God. With the cross in view, we can believe that God's love rules over all, and causes *"...all things to work together for good to those who love God, to those who are called according to His purpose"* (Romans 8:28).

Bible verse for devotion:

Jeremiah 10:23 –Who orders and directs your life?

Chapter 30

Miracles

Miracles are an instances of God's providence which has special relation to us or makes a peculiar impression on us.

- Miracles are instances of God's special providence.
- It is special in respect to the effect produced upon us.
- They are but a more impressive display of God's control.
- Miracles confirm to us that God is always on His throne.

Miracles are not to be regarded as belonging to a different order of things from God's general providences. Miracles just more readily suggest their divine authorship.

Miracles are often seen in Scripture as a response to prayer. God answers prayer with both spiritual and physical means. The realm of spirit is no less subject to God than the realm of matter.

Human minds can't grasp the operations of the wonder working God. The providential acts of God may be provided for in His prearrangement of the laws of the material universe and His decree of all the events of history. Because God is immanent in nature, His intervention through natural law may be as real a revelation of His personal care as if the laws of nature were suspended, and God interposed by an exercise of His creative power. However, God is not confined to nature or its laws. God can work by His creative and omnipotent will where other means are not sufficient.

In Scripture, miracles have a way of arresting our minds and hearts. They are often manifested in special times of God's deliverance and self-revelation, as evidenced in the lives of Moses, Elijah and Elisha, Jesus and His apostles.

> *Just as a father has compassion on his children, so the LORD has compassion on those who fear Him. For He Himself knows our frame; He is mindful that we are but dust.*
> **–Psalm 103:13-14**

God usually guides us, not by continual miracles, but by His natural providence and the energizing of our faculties by His Spirit, so that we rationally and freely do our own work, and yet fulfill His purpose.

God is continually near to His people by His providential working. God's providential working is perfectly adjusted to the Christian's nature and necessities. It is designed to give us instruction with regard to our duty and discipline to our moral character. It is also for our help and comfort in trials.

In interpreting God's providences, as in interpreting Scripture, we are dependent upon the Holy Spirit. The work of the Spirit is, in great part, an application of Scripture truth to present circumstances. The Holy Spirit gives our understanding of circumstances a fine sense of God's providential purposes with regard to us, although we may not always be able to explain it to others.

Miracles reveal God's special care for us. Miracles remind us of God's greatness. 1 Samuel 14:6 says *"...for the LORD is not restrained to save by many or by few."*

Bible verses for devotion:

Jn. 11:45-48 –How do miracles affect people?

Chapter 31

Angels and Demons

Angels are ministers of divine providence. God created angels as free spiritual beings. Good angels positively serve God's purpose by holiness and voluntary execution of His will. Fallen angels negatively serve God's purpose by giving examples to us of defeated and punished rebellion, and by illustrating God's distinguishing grace in our salvation.

- Angels were all created as holy, finite, personal spirits.
- Some preserved their integrity, others rebelled and fell.
- Voluntarily or involuntarily, they serve God's purpose.

Like miracles, angelic appearances generally mark God's entrance upon new epochs in the unfolding of His plans. We read of angels at completion of creation (Job 38:7); at the Fall (Gen. 3:24); at the giving of the law (Gal. 3:19); at the incarnation (Lu. 2:13); in the wild and in Gethsemane (Mat. 4:11, Lu. 22:43); at the resurrection (Mat. 28:2); at the ascension (Acts 1:10); and at the final judgment (Mat. 5:31).

Good angels are not to be considered as the mediating agents of God's regular and common providence, but as the ministers of His special providence in caring for His people. Their intervention is apparently occasional and exceptional, not at their own option, but only as it is commanded by God.

Good angels are represented as worshiping before God, watching over God's people and punishing God's enemies.

Evil angels oppose God and strive to defeat His will. This is indicated in the names applied to their chief. The word "Satan" means "adversary" - primarily to God, secondarily to men. Likewise, the term "devil" signifies "slanderer" of God to men (Genesis 3:1, 4), and of men to God (Rev. 12:10).

> *For He will give His angels charge concerning you, to guard you in all your ways. They will bear you up in their hands, that you do not strike your foot against a stone.*
> **–Psalm 91:11-12**

Yet, in spite of themselves, they execute God's plans of punishing the ungodly, of chastening the good, and of illustrating the nature and fate of moral evil.

The power of evil spirits over men is not independent of the human will. This power cannot be exercised without at least the original consent of man's will, and may be resisted and shaken off through prayer and faith in God. God's Spirit dwells in believers as their seal and guarantee (2 Cor. 1:22). He stands with us to plead God's cause with us and our cause with God (Jn. 16:8; Rom. 8:26). Even the angels marvel at our redemption in Christ (1 Pet. 1:12; Eph. 3:10; 1 Cor. 4:9).

The power of evil angels is also limited, both in time and in extent, by the permissive will of God. Evil spirits are neither omnipotent, omniscient, nor omnipresent.

Opposed to God as evil spirits are, God compels them to serve His purposes. Their power for harm lasts but for a season, and their ultimate judgment and punishment will vindicate God's permission of their evil agency.

Bible verses for devotion:

Hebrews 2:14; Colossians 2:15; 1 John 3:8–What victory was secured by Christ's death?

V. DOCTRINE OF MAN AND THE FALL

Chapter 32

Man as a Creation of God

God created man. Man was created for a unique relationship to God and the rest of creation.

- Man exists because of the creative act of God.
- The creation of man can't be explained apart from God.
- God created man to be different from all His creation.
- Man is the crown of all created things.

The fact of man's creation is declared in Genesis. Genesis 2:7 states *"Then the LORD God formed man of dust from the ground, and breathed into his nostrils the breath of life; and man became a living being."*

In the above passage, Scripture presents the soul as God breathed. It is an immediate creation of God.

Likewise, the forming of man's body is mentioned by the Scripture in direct connection with this creation of the spirit, presenting man's body as an immediate creation as well.

The Scriptures negate the idea that man is the mere product of unreasoning natural forces. Scripture refers man's existence to a cause different from mere nature, namely, the creative act of God.

The Scriptures presents man as the pinnacle of His creation, distinct in both likeness and position from all creation. Man was created to be very different from and above all other creatures and things.

Genesis 1:26 says *"Then God said, Let Us make man in Our image, according to Our likeness; and let them rule over the fish of the sea and over the birds of the sky and over the cattle and over all the earth, and over every creeping thing that creeps on the earth."*

> **Know that the Lord Himself is God; it is He who has made us, and not we ourselves; we are His people and the sheep of His pasture.** –Psalm 100:3

Man is unique among creatures in that he is created in the image of God. Reflecting God's nature and attributes, man has the capacity to relate with God. We will discuss this further in a later chapter when we study man's orignal state.

Reason points out the radical differences between man's soul and the priciple of intelligence in the lower animals. Man is man because his free will transcends the limitations of the brute creature. Man's possesion of self-consciouness, general ideas, the moral sense, and the power of self-determination show that man could not have been derived by any natural process of development from inferior creatures.

Job 32:8 illustrates this reasoning, telling us *"But it is a spirit in man, and the breath of the Almighty gives them understanding."*

Man is uniquely created by God to reflect His holiness and to bring Him glory. We were made to *"Exalt the Lord our God, and worship at His holy hill; for holy is the Lord our God"* (Ps. 99:9).

Bible verses for devotion:

Psalm 8:3-9–What are we crowned with? What is our dominion? Why? What for?

Chapter 33

Man as a Child of God

> *God is the Father of all men in that He originates and sustains them as personal beings like in nature to Him. Man's natural sonship underlies the history of the Fall and qualifies the doctrine of Sin.*

- God is Father to all men in only the rudimentary sense.
- We are naturally His children as all are created by Christ.
- We are spiritually His sons only as we are created anew.

In Luke 3:38, Adam is said to be "*...the son of God*" because God created him. Paul echoes this in Acts 17:28 telling the pagans "*...For we are also His children.*"

Jesus, in His parable of the prodigal son (Luke 15:11-32), portrays the father as father even before the prodigal returns.

God's natural fatherhood is mediated by Jesus Christ. Col. 1:16-17 teaches that "*...all things have been created through Him and for Him. He is before all things, and in Him all things hold together.*" All things created includes the creation of man, the crown of God's created order.

John 15:6 records Jesus saying "*If anyone does not abide in Me, he is thrown away as a branch and dries up; and they gather them, and cast them into the fire and they are burned.*" Here, Christ's words imply a natural union of all men with Christ. Otherwise, they would teach that those who are spiritually united to Him can perish everlastingly.

Fatherhood, in this larger sense, implies origination, impartation of life and likeness in faculties and powers.

Fatherhood also implies God's sustentation, government, care and love of His creation.

God's fatherhood is evidenced in His fatherly treatment of man and in His universal claim on man for filial love and trust (Mat. 23:9).

> *Do we not all have one father? Has not one God created us? Why do we deal treacherously each against his brother so as to profane the covenant of our fathers?*
> *—Malachi 2:10*

God's fatherhood makes incarnation possible, for this implies oneness of nature between God and man. The atoning death of Christ could be effective only upon the ground of a common nature in Christ and in humanity. Even the regenerating work of the Holy Spirit is intelligible only as the restoration of a filial relation which was native to man, but which his sin had disrupted.

This natural fatherhood, therefore, prepares the way for God's special Fatherhood toward those who have been regenerated by His Spirit and who have believed on His Son.

All are naturally sons of God. But not all are spiritually sons of God. Many are *"children of wrath"* (Ephesians 2:3) and *"perdition"* (John 17:12).

God is spiritually the Father only of those renewed by His Spirit. Only those who have joined themselves by faith to Christ have *"...received a Spirit of adoption as sons by which we cry out, "Abba! Father!"* (Rom. 8:15).

Bible verses for devotion:

Galatians 4:1-7 –What does our adoption imply?

Chapter 34

Unity of the Human Race

The Scriptures teach that the whole human race is descended from a single pair.

- This truth is basic to the unity of humanity in the first sin.
- This is basic to the provision of man's salvation in Christ.
- This constitutes the basis of man's obligation to man.

Genesis 1:27-28 clearly details the beginning of man, saying *"God created man in His own image; in the image of God He created him; male and female He created them. God blessed them; and God said to them: Be fruitful and multiply, and fill the earth and subdue it..."*

Genesis 3:20 records *"Now the man called his wife's name Eve, because she was the mother of all the living."*

The testimony of Genesis teaches that all of humanity shares a common family tree.

The organic unity of the human race is at the heart of Paul's teaching concerning the unity of mankind in the first transgression. Paul writes in Romans 5:12 *"Therefore, just as through one man sin entered the world, and death through sin, and so death spread to all men, because all sinned."* Paul further elaborates this truth in Rom. 5:19 stating that by *"...one man's disobedience the many were made sinners..."*

The unity of mankind that causes all to share in Adam's transgression, also makes it possible for sin's curse to be lifted through the work of Jesus Christ.

1 Corinthians 15:21-22 instructs us that *"For since by a man came death, by a Man also came the resurrection of the dead. For as in Adam all die, so also in Christ all will be made alive."*

> *And He made from one man every nation of mankind to live on all the face of the earth...*
> **–Acts 17:26**

This is God's gracious provision for the salvation of man. Paul expounds on this gracious provision in Romans 5:17 saying *"For if by the transgression of the one, death reigned through the one, much more those who receive the abundance of grace and of the gift of righteousness will reign in life through the One, Jesus Christ."*

The descent of humanity from a single pair also forms the ground of man's obligation of natural brotherhood to every member of the race. 1 Jn. 3:17 asks if a man denies a *"...brother in need...how does the love of God abide in him?"*

The writer of Hebrews 2:11-12 describes this natural brotherhood, declaring *"For both He who sanctifies and those who are sanctified are all from one Father; for which reason He is not ashamed to call them brethren, saying: I will proclaim Your name to My brethren, In the midst of the congregation I will sing Your praise."*

The common heritage of mankind is foundational to understanding man's participation in sin, God's gracious offer of redemption through the work of Christ, and both our rationale and responsibility of being our brother's keeper.

Bible verses for devotion:

Hebrews 2:16-17 –Who is included as a *"descendant of Abraham"*? Who are *"His brethren"*? What does this teach us?

Chapter 35

Man's Essential Makeup

Man has a two-fold nature, both material and immaterial. Man consists of body and soul (or spirit).

- Man is composed of two parts, body and soul.
- Man's two parts form an organic unity, a whole man.

The two elements in man's being is a fact to which consciousness testifies. Man is as conscious that his immaterial part is a unity, as that his body is a unity. He knows two, and only two, parts of his being — body and soul.

This testimony is confirmed by Scripture, in the account of man's creation. Gen. 2:7 says *"And the LORD God formed man of the dust of the ground, and breathed into his nostrils the breath of life; and man became a living being* (soul)."

Scripture is careful to distinguish the soul (or spirit) of man from the body which it inhabits. Ecclesiastes 12:7 says *"Then the dust will return to the earth as it was, and the spirit will return to God who gave it."* James 2:26 teaches that *"...the body without the spirit is dead..."*

Likewise, Scripture is careful to distinguish the spirit of man from the Spirit of God. One such example is Numbers 16:22, which calls God the *"...God of the spirits of all flesh..."* Another such passage is Zechariah 12:1, which exalts *"...the LORD who...forms the spirit of man within him."*

The terms soul and spirit are used interchangeably in Scripture. For example, *"his spirit was troubled"* (Gen. 41:8); *"my soul is in despair within me."* (Ps. 42:6); *"Now My soul has become troubled"* (Jn. 12:27); *"He became troubled in spirit..."* (Jn. 13:21).

> **The LORD heard the voice of Elijah, and the life of the child returned to him, and he revived.**
> **–1 Kings 17:22**

This is especially common in the Old Testament.

Although the terms soul and spirit are often used interchangeably, and always designate the same substance, they are sometimes employed as contrasting terms.

Some Scriptures, such as 1 Thessalonians 5:23 and Hebrews 4:12, seem to differentiate soul and spirit as constituting different parts of man's immaterial makeup. On closer inspection, we find that the verses simply highlight the whole of the soul and all of its relations. These verses do not designate a separate part of immaterial man any more than Jesus's command in Mark 12:30 to *"love the LORD your God with all your heart, with all your soul, with all your mind, and with all your strength."* Here, Jesus is not teaching a four part makeup of man. He only refers to man's entirety.

Although man is represented as having a two-fold nature, man is related to as an organic unity, a whole man. It is man who transgresses and is accountable to God, not his soul or body independently.

In Mat. 10:28, Jesus taught us to fear God *"...who is able to destroy both soul and body in hell."* Graciously, Christ's provision and offer of salvation for man is presented for the whole man, both body and soul.

Bible verse for devotion:

Psalm 139:14 –How are you made?

Chapter 36

Man's Conscience

Conscience is the moral judiciary of the soul. It is the power within us of judgment and command.

- Conscience must judge according to the law given to it.
- Its decisions are based on the moral standard you accept.
- Its decisions are as just as the moral reason it is based on.

The office of conscience is to 'bear witness'. Romans 2:15 teaches that men "...*show the work of the Law written in their hearts, their conscience bearing witness and their thoughts alternately accusing or else defending them.*"

Conscience does not furnish the law, but it bears witness with the law which is furnished by other sources. This explains how men are bound to follow their consciences and yet at the same time, their consciences can differ so greatly.

Conscience is uniform and infallible in the sense that it always decides rightly according to the law given it. Men's decisions vary because moral reason presents to the conscience different standards by which to judge.

This moral reason may become depraved by sin, so that the light becomes darkness (Mat. 6:22-23) and conscience has only a perverse standard by which to judge. The weak conscience (1 Cor. 8:12) is one whose standard of judgment is yet imperfect. The conscience 'branded' or "*seared...as with a branding iron*" (1 Tim. 4:2) is one whose standard has been wholly perverted by practical disobedience.

The word of God and the Holy Spirit are the chief agencies in rectifying our standards of judgment. They enable our conscience to make absolutely right decisions.

> *Your word I have treasured in my heart, that I might not sin against You.*
> **–Psalm 119:11**

God can so unite the soul to Christ that it becomes partaker of His satisfaction to justice and is thus *"...sprinkled clean from an evil conscience..."* (Heb. 10:22). As we experience His sanctifying power, our conscience is thus enabled to obey God's command and to speak of a *"good conscience"* (1 Pet. 3:16, 21) instead of an *"evil conscience"* (Heb. 10:22) or a conscience *"defiled"* (Titus 1:15) by sin.

The conscience of the regenerate man may have such right standards, and its decisions may be followed by such uniformly right action, that its voice, though it is not itself God's voice, is yet the very echo of God's voice.

The renewed conscience may take up into itself and express the witness of the Holy Spirit. Paul confirms this, saying that his conscience *"...testifies with me in the Holy Spirit"* (Romans 9:1).

Conscience is not an original authority. It points to something higher than itself. This authority of conscience is simply the authority of the moral law, or rather the authority of the personal God, whose nature the law is but a transcript.

Conscience, therefore, with its continual and supreme demand that the right should be done, furnishes the best witness to man of the existence of a personal God, and of the supremacy of holiness in Him in whose image we are made.

Bible verse for devotion:

1 Jn. 3:20 – How can a weak conscience mislead us?

Chapter 37

Man's Will

Will is the soul's power to choose between motives, determining both an end and the means to attain it.

- God created man with the ability to make moral choices.
- With will comes responsibility.
- Man's ability to choose is real, but self-limited.

The reasoning of our minds and the desires of our hearts present our souls with motives. Our motives often conflict, prompting the will to choose between motives. Man's will embraces his thoughts and passions and directs his activities.

Man has the power to make individual decisions in a direction opposite to his current motive and course. This is the power of a contrary choice.

Man's will is truly free. Man's will is not determined by motives acting upon his will.

Motives are not causes, which compel the will, but influences which persuade it. Man has power to change these motives and act contrary to them.

Denial that the will is free has serious and damaging consequences in theology. Its denial weakens, if not destroys a man's conviction with regard to responsibility, sin, guilt and retribution, and thus the need of atonement.

Its denial also weakens, if not destroys a man's faith in his own power as well as in God's power of initiating action, and so obscures the very possibility of atonement.

Man's will is free, but its freedom is self-limited. Man's willful acts form a bend in his will which directs his future acts.

> *...for the willing is present in me...*
> **–Romans 7:18**

Every decision of the will turns our thought either toward or away from an object of desire, creating a path upon which future thoughts may easily travel. With repeated acts of will in a given moral direction, the affections may become so confirmed in evil or in good as to almost make certain the future good or evil action of the man.

Therefore, while the will is free, the man may either be a *"slave of sin"* (John 8:34) or be counted among the *"slaves of righteousness"* (Romans 6:18) and the *"righteous made perfect"* (Hebrews 12:23).

Man's will is corrupted by sin. This sinful bent of the will toward evil becomes so constant and settled that man cannot by a single act reverse his moral state. In this respect man has not the power of a contrary choice. He can change his character only indirectly, by turning his attention to considerations fitted to awaken opposite dispositions, and by thus summoning up motives to an opposite course.

Studying the action of the sinful will alone, one might conclude that there is no such thing as freedom. But our consciousness testifies to freedom. Consciousness must be trusted, though we cannot reconcile the two. The will is as great a mystery as is the doctrine of the Trinity.

Scripture reveals most clearly the degradation of our will. Yet it also discloses the remedy. John 8:36 says *"So if the Son makes you free, you will be free indeed."*

Bible verse for devotion:

Phil. 4:13 –What happens when God energizes the will of man?

Chapter 38

Man's Original State

Man was created in the image of God. This image consists in both man's natural likeness and in his moral likeness to God.

- God created man to reflect His nature or personality.
- God created man to reflect His moral attributes.
- God created man to walk in holiness.

Genesis 1:27 says God created man *"in His own image"*. God created man in His likeness to be a personal being, both self-conscious and self-determining. This means that man reflects, wills and acts from within by virtue of his free will.

By virtue of this personality, man could at his creation choose which of the objects of his knowledge (self, the world, or God) should be the norm and center of his development.

The possession of natural likeness to God, or personality, involves boundless possibilities of good or ill.

This natural likeness to God is inalienable. It constitutes a capacity for redemption that gives value to the life even of the unregenerate (Genesis 9:6; James 3:9; 1 Peter 2:17).

Indeed it constitutes the reason why Christ should die. Man was worth redeeming. The lost sheep, the lost piece of money, and the lost son were worth the effort to seek and to save (Luke 15). Christ's death for man revealed the infinite worth of the human soul, and taught us to count all men as brethren for whose salvation we may well give up our lives.

God created man with a direction of the affections and the will to reflect His moral likeness. Since holiness is the fundamental attribute of God, this must of necessity be

> *Behold, I have found only this, that God made men upright...*
> **–Ecclesiastes 7:29**

the chief attribute of His image in the moral beings whom He creates (Ephesians 4:24; Colossians 3:8-10).

Newly created man had right moral tendencies, as well as freedom from actual fault. Otherwise the communion with God described in Genesis would not have been possible.

Though the first man was fundamentally good, he still had the power of choosing evil. There was a bent of the affections and will toward God, but man was not yet confirmed in holiness.

The loss of this moral likeness to God was the chief calamity of the Fall. Man has defaced the image of God in his nature, even though that image, in its natural aspect, is enduring. As Pascal said, man is now both "the glory and the scandal of the universe."

The dignity of human nature consists, not so much in what man is, but in what God meant him to be, and in what God means him yet to become when the lost image of God is restored by the union of man's soul with Christ. Because of his future possibilities, the lowest of mankind is sacred.

The great sin of the second table of the Decalogue is the sin of despising our fellow man. To harbor and cherish contempt for others can have its root only in idolatry, self and rebellion against God.

Bible verse for devotion:

Gen. 1:31 –How does God describe man at creation?

Chapter 39

The Law of God

The law of God is an expression of the moral nature of God, and therefore of God's holiness. It requires man's absolute conformity to His holiness. Man fulfills the law only as he becomes a finite image of God's infinite perfections.

- The whole law may be summed up as: "Be like God."

The law of God is simply an expression of the nature of God in the form of moral requirement. As a revelation of God's holiness, the law of God is His face disclosed to human sight. The perfect embodiment and fulfillment of this law is seen only in Jesus Christ (Romans 10:4).

We should not say that God makes law, nor on the other hand that God is subject to law, but rather that God is law and the source of law. The law of God is not an arbitrary act of His will. Moral law extends from the being of God.

Law, then, has a deeper foundation than that God merely "said so". As God's word and God's will are revelations of His inmost being, His law is but a transcript of His holy nature. Every transgression of the law is a stab at the heart of God.

The obligation to obey His law and to be conformed to God's perfect moral character is based upon man's original ability and the gifts which God bestowed upon him at the beginning. Man, created in the image of God, has the duty to render back to God that which God first gave him.

God requires perfect holiness in man as the condition of harmony with His own infinite holiness. To let down this standard would be to misrepresent Himself.

God's law is not a sliding scale of requirements which adapts to its subjects. God Himself can't change it without ceasing to be God.

> *For the law was given through Moses; grace and truth were realized through Jesus Christ.*
> **—John 1:17**

Some laws in the Bible differ in that they are ceremonial or special injunctions from God, being temporary in nature. An example of this is the dietary laws of Israel. Such modes of expression, like the Mosaic system, may be abolished, but the essential demands are unchanging (Matthew 5:17-18). Issued by God for spiritual tutelage, He alone can say when they cease to be binding upon us in their outward form.

Only to the first man was the law proposed as a method of salvation. With the first sin, all hope of obtaining the divine favor by perfect obedience is lost. God's law reminds man of the heights from which he has fallen and drives him to Christ for righteousness and salvation (Romans 8:3-4).

Man needs law, just as railway cars need a track to guide them. To leap the track is to find, not freedom, but ruin.

Thus, God's law both demands and protects. The law is thus not only for ownership, but also for care. Law is God's transcript of holiness as well as a partial revelation of His everlasting love.

It is in grace that we find the chief revelation of His love. Love saves not by ignoring law, but in satisfying its demands.

Bible verse for devotion:

Galatians 3:24–What is the purpose of the Law?

Chapter 40

The Nature of Sin

Sin is the lack of conformity to the moral law of God, either in act, disposition, or state.

- Sin is not just an act or transgression of the law.
- Sin is a principle of opposition to God.
- Sin's essence always and everywhere is selfishness.

Sin is falling short of God's holy perfection. When we break His commandments, we fail to conform to His nature.

Sin is more than just an external action. Romans 14:23 declares "*...whatever is not from faith is sin.*" Ja. 4:17 states "*...to one who knows the right thing to do and does not do it, to him it is sin.*" The Bible speaks of "*evil thoughts*" (Mat. 15:19) and an "*evil heart*" (Heb. 3:12). Such inclinations show that sin, like an iceberg, lies deep below the surface.

Sin is a state of unlikeness to God. It is a depravity of the affections and a perversion of the will, which constitutes man's inmost character. As God's holiness is not passive purity but purity willing, so sin is not passive impurity but is impurity willing. This corruption steers and masters the soul.

All sin is either explicit or implicit hostility against God (Romans 8:7). All true confessions, like David's in Psalm 51:4, say "*Against You, You only, I have sinned, and done what is evil in Your sight...*" It might be said of every sinner that they "*...Do not fight with small or great, but with the king of Israel alone*" (1 Kings 22:31).

Not every sinner is conscious of this enmity. But this indifference easily grows in the presence of threatening and penalty into violent hatred to God and positive defiance of His law. If the sin which is now hidden in the sinner's heart were but permitted to develop

> *Everyone who practices sin also practices lawlessness; and sin is lawlessness.*
> **−1 John 3:4**

itself according to its own nature, it would attempt to hurl the Almighty from His throne and set up its own kingdom.

Sin desires to obliterate God and His works, which testify of Him (Romans 1).

Selfishness is the essence of sin. Just as God makes His holiness the central thing, so we are to live for that, loving self only in God and for God's sake. This love for God as holy is the essence of virtue. The opposite of this is the supreme love for self, which is sin.

Sin chooses self instead of God as the object of affection and the supreme end of being. Man ought to make God the center of his life, surrendering himself unconditionally to God and possessing himself only in subordination to God's will. Instead, the sinner makes himself the center of his life. Man sets his own interest as the supreme motive and his will as the supreme rule. Man sets himself directly against God.

Side by side with the selfish will, and striving against it, is the Spirit of Christ, the immanent God, imparting aspirations and impulses foreign to unregenerate humanity. This prepares the way for the soul's surrender to truth and righteousness. These impulses to righteousness stem not from man, but from Christ moving man to seek salvation.

Bible verse for devotion:

Lk. 5:8–Was Peter confessing a single sin or a state?

Chapter 41

The Universality of Sin

All men have consciously committed acts or cherished dispositions that are contrary to the moral law of God. These sinful acts and dispositions are the result of man's universally corrupt nature.

- There is no one without sin.
- All are born with a corrupt state.
- From this state, sinful acts and dispositions flow.

The truth that all of humanity have sinned is found throughout Scripture. In the Old Testament, 1 Kings 8:46 says *"...there is no man who does not sin..."* Ps. 143:2 pleads *"Do not enter into judgment with Your servant, for in Your sight no man living is righteous."* Pr. 20:9 asks *"Who can say, I have cleansed my heart, I am pure from my sin?"* Eccl. 7:20 declares *"Indeed, there is not a righteous man on earth who continually does good and who never sins."*

The New Testament teaches the universality of sin in Luke 11:13, stating *"If you then, being evil..."* Rom. 3:10, 12 says *"There is none righteous, not even one...There is none who does good...."* Gal. 3:22 shows *"...Scripture has shut up everyone under sin..."* James 3:2 remarks *"For we all stumble in many things..."* 1 Jn. 1:8 instructs *"If we say that we have no sin, we are deceiving ourselves and the truth is not in us."* Jesus taught all men to pray in Mat. 6:12 saying *"...forgive us our debts..."* Mat. 6:14 confirms our need for forgiveness and bids us to *"...forgive others..."* as well.

The sinful acts and dispositions of men stem from man's corrupt nature. This nature is an inborn corrupt state from which sin flows. This nature is in mind when Jesus states in Luke 6:45 "...*the evil man out of the evil treasure* (of his heart) *brings forth evil.*" In Mat. 12:34, Jesus says "*You brood of vipers, how can you, being evil, speak what is good?*" Ps. 58:3 traces this state back to birth saying "*The wicked are estranged from the womb; these who speak lies go astray from birth.*"

> *For all have sinned and fall short of the glory of God.*
> –**Romans 3:23**

Ps. 51:5 states "*Behold, I was brought forth in iniquity, and in sin my mother conceived me.*" Here, David confesses not his mother's sin, but his own sin. He teaches that man himself is sinful before God from his birth, before his works.

Ephesians 2:3 declares all men to be "...*by nature children of wrath...*" Nature here signifies something inborn and original as distinguished from that which is acquired subsequently. This text implies that: (a) Sin is a nature in the sense of an inherited depravity of the will. (b) This nature is guilty and condemnable. (c) All men share in this nature and in this consequent guilt and condemnation.

When a man says he is unconscious of any sin, it is only proof that he is a great and hardened transgressor. Denial of sin is damning because if one never realizes his sin, there is no salvation.

Opposed to this, we see the amazing grace of God. This grace is manifested not only in the gift of Christ to die for sinners, but in the gift of the Holy Spirit to convince men of their sins and to lead them to accept the Savior.

Bible verse for devotion:

Psalm 90:8–How are our sins brought to light?

Chapter 42

The Fall of Man

The Fall of Man is found in the free act of Adam and Eve by which they turned away from God, corrupted themselves, and brought themselves under the penalties of the law.

- The account of the man's fall is found in Genesis 3:1-7.
- Man alone is responsible for his sin.

In Genesis 3:1, Satan tempts Eve with appeals to innocent appetites, along with the implication that God was arbitrarily withholding the means of their gratification.

Eve sinned by isolating herself and choosing to seek her own pleasure without regard to God's will. This initial selfishness led her to listen to the tempter instead of rebuking him or fleeing from him. It even led her to exaggerate God's command as recorded in Genesis 3:3.

In Gen. 3:4-5, Satan denied the truthfulness of God. He charged the Almighty of jealousy and fraud in keeping His creatures in a position of ignorance and dependence.

Eve chose not to believe God and willfully began to cherish the desire for the forbidden fruit as a means of independence and knowledge. Thus unbelief, pride, and lust all sprang from man's desire to serve himself (Gen. 3:6).

Man's heart and its desires became corrupt. The inward disposition openly manifested itself. Gen. 3:6 says both Eve and Adam sinned. Adam shared in Eve's choice and longing.

Thus man fell inwardly, before the outward act of eating the forbidden fruit. He fell in that one fundamental determination whereby he made the supreme choice of self instead of God.

> *The serpent said to the woman: You surely will not die!*
> **–Genesis 3:4**

Man denied God's absolute ownership and asserted his own. Sin revealed a will thoroughly corrupted and alienated from God.

Man should have known evil as God knows it- as a thing possible, hateful, and forever rejected. But man learned to know evil as Satan knows it- by making it actual. It was a bitter experience resulting in physical and spiritual death.

We can't understand how the first unholy emotion could have dwelt in a mind that was set supremely upon God.

We can't grasp how temptation could overcome a soul in which there were no unholy tendencies to which it could appeal. The power of choice doesn't explain unholy choice.

We can't dismiss the fall as only a deception of our first parents by Satan. Their very yielding to such deception presupposes distrust of God and alienation from Him.

Sin exists. God is not its author. God cannot be sin's author, either by creating man's nature so that sin was a necessary incident of its development, or by withdrawing a supernatural grace which was necessary to keep man holy.

We must accept the Scripture doctrine that sin originated in man's free act of revolt from God. It was the act of a will which, though inclined toward God, was not yet confirmed in virtue and was still capable of a contrary choice.

Bible verse for devotion:

Genesis 3:15–How does God make provision our sin?

Chapter 43

Original Sin

The origin of our sinful nature is found in the sin of our first parents. When Adam and Eve rebelled against God, our common nature was corrupted and depravity, guilt and penalty came to all humanity.

- All men since Adam have been born in a sinful state.
- Adam's sin is the direct cause and ground of depravity.
- In Adam, men are thus depraved, guilty and condemned.

Scripture states that the transgression of our first parents made all their descendants sinners. Rom. 5:19 says by "...*one man's disobedience the many were made sinners...*"

Adam's sin is imputed, reckoned, or charged to every member of the race, of which he was the head. Romans 5:16 states "...*the judgment arose from one transgression resulting in condemnation...*" In Adam, we are all born depraved and are thus "...*by nature children of wrath...*" (Ephesians 2:3).

Two questions arise from this teaching. First, how can we be responsible for a depraved nature which we did not personally and consciously originate? Secondly, how can God justly charge to us the sin of the first father of the race?

These questions are substantially the same. 1 Cor. 15:22 intimates the true answer to the problem declaring that "...*in Adam all die...*" Likewise, Rom. 5:12 teaches "...*through one man sin entered into the world, and death through sin, and so death spread to all men, because all sinned.*"

In other words, Adam's sin is the root and basis of the depravity, guilt, and condemnation of all humanity. This is simply because Adam and his offspring are one by virtue of their organic unity. Thus, the sin of Adam is the sin of the race. Adam and his progeny share the same evil nature.

> *...through one man sin entered into the world, and death through sin, and so death spread to all men...*
> **–Romans 5:12**

Humanity's common fallen nature is self-corrupted and averse to God. This nature manifests itself in our own personal transgressions, just as it did in Adam's. We are not sinners merely because God regards and treats us as such. God regards us as sinners because we are sinners.

In attempts to explain God's justice in imputing to us the sin of our first father, many theories have been devised. We acknowledge that no human theory can fully untangle the mystery of imputation. Our finite minds can't solve the dark problem of a corruption which is inborn yet condemnable.

Yet this is a central fact that is taught in Scripture. We feel compelled to believe upon divine testimony, even though our attempted explanation should prove unsatisfactory. This truth should lead us to acknowledge the depths of our soul's ruin and our absolute dependence upon God for salvation.

We would be remiss to forget that there is also a physical and natural union with Christ which precedes the fall and results from the creation of man. This immanence of Christ in humanity guarantees a continuous divine effort to remedy the disaster caused by man's free will, and to restore the holy union with God for which the race was created, but has lost.

Bible verses for devotion:

Rom. 5:12-18; 1 Cor. 15:21-22–Consider God's grace.

Chapter 44

Depravity

Depravity is the lack of original righteousness and holy affection toward God. It is also the corruption of man's moral nature with a bias toward evil.

- It is the absence of love and of moral likeness to God.
- It is the presence of manifold tendencies to evil.

When man first came from the hand of God, it was his nature to fear, love, and trust God above all things. This tendency toward God was lost in the fall of man. Sin has altered and defiled man's innermost nature (Titus 1:15-16). In place of this bent to God, there's now a fearful bent to evil.

The Scriptures represent human nature as totally depraved. This doesn't mean that man is absolutely demonic, destitute of conscience, devoid of any human good, prone to every sin, and utmost in selfishness and opposition to God.

Total depravity means that the sinner's bent toward evil disorders and corrupts his entire person. Man's whole life, inward and outward, is determined by a preference of self to God. Man is totally destitute of the love of God (John 5:42).

Depravity is not just being deprived of good. Depravity is more than deprivation. It is evil embraced. An evil man will spiral downward (2 Tim. 3:13). By God's grace alone, the divine influence within can quicken a man's conscience and kindle aspirations for better things. The immanent Christ is "....*the true Light which, coming into the world, enlightens every man*" (John 1:9).

"For it is by grace you have been saved, through faith – and this is not from yourselves, it is the gift of God – not by works, so that no one can boast."

No man can of himself change the underlying corrupt state of his affections and will. The sinner cannot by a single act of will bring his character and life to conform to God's law (Eph. 2:8-10).

> *For we know that the Law is spiritual, but I am of flesh, sold into bondage to sin.*
> –Romans 7:14

Depraved men are described in Eph. 4:18-19 as *"being darkened in their understanding, excluded from the life of God because of the ignorance that is in them, because of the hardness of their heart; and they, having become callous, have given themselves over to sensuality for the practice of every kind of impurity with greediness."* Inability results from sin and is itself sin.

Yet there is a certain remnant of freedom left to man. There are degrees of depravity. The sinner can choose the less sin rather than the greater. He can refuse altogether to yield to certain temptations. He can do outwardly good acts, though with imperfect motives. He can even seek God from motives of self-interest, opening himself to divine influence. Freedom of choice, within this limit, is not incompatible with complete bondage of the will in spiritual things (Jn. 1:12-13).

Over against total depravity, we must set total redemption. Over against original sin, we must set original grace. Christ is in every human heart mitigating the effects of sin, urging all to repentance, and is *"...able to save forever those who draw near to God through Him..."* (Heb. 7:25). Even the unregenerate heathen may put off *"...the old self..."* and *"...put on the new self..."* (Eph. 4:22, 24), being delivered from *"...the body of this death...through Jesus Christ our Lord"* (Rom. 7:24, 25).

Bible verse for devotion:

Romans 7:18–What good does Paul find in man?

Chapter 45

Guilt

Guilt is humanity's merit of punishment. It is man's obligation to render satisfaction to God's justice for the sins he has committed.

- The holiness of God demands absolute conformity.
- Sin is an affront to the holiness of God.

There is a reaction of holiness against sin, which the Scripture denominates "...*the wrath of God...*" (Rom. 1:18). God's punitive righteousness is over against the sinner, as something to be feared. Guilt is thus a relation of the sinner to God's righteousness, namely man's desert of punishment.

Guilt is not mere liability to punishment without participation in the transgression. We are guilty only of that sin which we have originated or have had part in originating. Guilt is incurred only through direct transgression either on the part of man's nature or person. We are accounted guilty for what we have done and for what we are in consequence.

It is customary to speak lightly of original sin, as if personal sins were all for which man is accountable. But it is only in the light of original sin that personal sins can be explained. Our personal transgression is but our conscious ratification and participation in Adam's rebellion. Our guilt lies in what we are, as much as for what we do.

Guilt is the objective result of sin (Rom. 3:19). Guilt is distinct from depravity, which is pollution resulting from sin.

Every sin, whether of nature or person, is an offense against God. It is an act or state of opposition to His will which has for its effect God's personal wrath (John 3:18, 36). Sin, as antagonism to God's holy will, involves guilt. This guilt, or obligation to satisfy the outraged

> *God is a righteous judge, and a God who has indignation every day.*
> **–Psalm 7:11**

holiness of God, is explained in Scripture by the terms "debtor" and "debt" (Mat. 6:12; Luke 11:4; Mat. 5:21; Rom. 6:23; Eph. 2:3).

Guilt and depravity are also separable in fact. Christians are free from guilt (Rom. 8:1), but not yet free from depravity (Rom. 7:23). Christ, on the other hand, was under obligation to suffer (Luke 24:26; Acts 3:18; 26:23), while yet He was without sin (Heb. 7:26). The necessity of Christ's suffering was not in the needs of man, but in the holiness of God.

The revulsion of God's holiness from sin, and its demand for satisfaction, are reflected in the shame and remorse of every awakened conscience. There is an instinct in man's heart that sin will be punished, and ought so to be. The Holy Spirit makes this so deeply felt that the soul has no rest until its debt is paid. So Jesus, when laden with the guilt of the race, pressed forward to the cross, saying: *"But I have a baptism to undergo, and how distressed I am until it is accomplished!"* (Luke 12:50; Mark 10:32).

This relation of sin to God shows us how Christ was made *"...to be sin on our behalf..."* (2 Cor. 5:21). For the very reason of His humanity, Christ bore in His own Person all the guilt of humanity and is *"...the Lamb of God who..."* takes, and so *"...takes away the sin of the world"* (Jn. 1:29).

Bible verses for devotion:

Hebrews 10:26-31–Consider those who reject Christ.

Chapter 46

Penalty

Penalty is the necessary reaction of the holiness of God against sin. Penalty is the vindication of the character of the Lawgiver.

- God must vindicate Himself or He ceases to be holy.
- Scripture designates the total penalty of sin as "death".

Penalty is vindicative, but not vindictive. The wrath of God is calm and judicial, devoid of all passion or caprice. It is the expression of eternal and unchangeable righteousness.

Natural consequences of transgression are a part of the penalty of sin. Sensual sins are punished in the deterioration and corruption of the body just as mental and spiritual sins deteriorate and corrupt the soul. Pr. 5:22 states *"His own iniquities will capture the wicked, and he will be held in the cords of his sin."* Sin is self-detecting and self-tormenting.

However, it would be an error to confine all penalty to the reaction of natural laws. Natural law is but only the regular expression of God's mind and will.

We must remember that God is not merely immanent in the universe, but is also transcendent. Penalty is to fall into the hands, not simply of the law, but also of the Lawgiver. Heb. 10:31 says *"It is a terrifying thing to fall into the hands of the living God."* God warns us in Jer. 44:4, *"Oh, do not do this abominable thing which I hate!"* There is no penalty of sin more dreadful than being an object of abhorrence to God.

The divine feeling toward sin is seen in Jesus' scourging the traffickers in the temple, His denunciation of the Pharisees, His weeping over Jerusalem, and His

> *For the wages of sin is death...*
> —**Romans 6:23**

agony in Gethsemane. Imagine a father's feeling toward his daughter's betrayer, and God's feeling toward sin may be faintly understood.

Punishment is essentially different from chastisement. Whereas chastisement proceeds from love (Jer. 10:24; Heb. 12:6), punishment proceeds not from love, but from justice. God's justice is offended by sin. Eze. 28:22 speaks of the vindication of His justice declaring "...*Thus says the* Lord *God: Behold, I am against you, O Sidon, and I will be glorified in your midst. Then they will know that I am the* Lord *when I execute judgments in her, and I will manifest my Holiness in her.*"

The penalty of sin is death. Death is both physical and spiritual. Physical death is the separation of the soul from the body. It includes all those temporal evils and physical sufferings which result from disturbing the original harmony between body and soul, which is the working of death in us.

Spiritual death is the chief part of the penalty of sin. It is the separation of the soul from God. It is the absence of that which constitutes the true life of the soul, the presence and favor of God. This death includes all that pain of conscience, loss of peace, and sorrow of spirit, which result from disturbing the normal relation between the soul and God.

Eternal death may be regarded as the culmination and completion of spiritual death (2 Thes. 1:8-9). By God's grace, this death is escaped by the Christian (John 11:25-26).

Bible verses for devotion:

    1 Cor. 15:53-56–Are you a victor in Christ over death?

Chapter 47

The Salvation of Infants

In Adam, all are born depraved and are subject to God's wrath. Yet infants are recognized in Scripture as having a relative innocence as they have not personally transgressed. Jesus employed infants to illustrate the trust and submission necessary for salvation. God's special compassion and care of infants gives us certainty of their salvation.

- Infants are in a state of sin and are saved only in Christ.

Job 14:4 asks *"Who can make the clean out of the unclean? No one!"* John 3:6 states *"That which is born of the flesh is flesh..."* Rom. 5:14 teaches *"Nevertheless death reigned from Adam to Moses, even over those who had not sinned in the likeness of the offense of Adam..."* Such verses highlight the sinful state of infants.

Jesus says in Mat. 19:14 *"...Let the little children alone, and do not hinder them from coming to Me..."* Here, Jesus confirms their need for salvation. Coming to Christ is always the coming of a sinner to Him who is the sacrifice for sin.

Scripture asserts that infants have not personally sinned. In Deut. 1:39, God refers to *"...your little ones...who this day have no knowledge of good and evil..."* Jonah 4:11 speaks of children *"...who do not know the difference between their right and left hand..."* Rom. 9:11 speaks of infants that are *"...not yet born and had not done anything good or bad..."* Their fallen nature hasn't yet manifested itself.

As certain and great as is the guilt of original sin, no human soul is eternally condemned solely for this sin of inherited nature. At the final judgment, personal conduct is made the test of character (Rev. 20:12-13). But infants are incapable of personal transgression. We have reason therefore to believe that they will be among the saved, since this rule of decision will not apply to them.

> *But now he has died; why should I fast? Can I bring him back again? I will go to him, but he will not return to me.*
> *—2 Sam. 12:23*

In Mat. 18:3-4, Jesus said *"Truly I say to you, unless you are converted and become like children, you will not enter the kingdom of heaven. Whoever then humbles himself as this child, he is the greatest in the kingdom of heaven."* The Savior's words do not intimate that little children are either sinless creatures, or subjects for baptism. Jesus is saying that their humble teachableness, intense eagerness, and simple trust illustrate the traits necessary for admission into the divine kingdom.

Jesus taught that infants are special objects of His care. Mat. 18:10 states *"See that you do not despise one of these little ones, for I say to you that their angels in heaven continually see the face of My Father who is in heaven."* Mat. 18:14 instructs *"So it is not the will of your Father who is in heaven that one of these little ones perish."*

The infants whom the Lord gathers together from this life are regenerated by the Holy Spirit likely in connection with the infant soul's first view of Christ. Their first moment of consciousness is only sweetness with Christ the Savior.

Bible verse for devotion:

1 John 3:2—Are you looking forward to seeing Jesus?

VI. JESUS CHRIST

Chapter 48

The Person of Christ

The redemption of mankind from sin was to be effected through a Mediator who should unite in Himself both the human nature and the divine, in order that He might reconcile God to man and man to God. This Mediator is Jesus Christ.

- Incarnation means "coming in flesh".
- Jesus Christ is God Incarnate.

God had from eternity decreed to redeem mankind. The history of the race from the Fall to the coming of Christ was providentially arranged to prepare the way for redemption.

Why could not Eve have been the mother of the chosen seed that would break the serpent's head (Gen. 3:15)? Eve likely at the first supposed that she was. Gen. 4:1 says "...*and she conceived and gave birth to Cain, and said, I have gotten a manchild with the help of the LORD.*" Some translators render it, "*I have gotten a man, even Jehovah.*" Why was not the cross set up at the gates of Eden?

Scripture intimates that a preparation was needful. God, in His wisdom and sovereignty, prepared the world for the coming of Christ. Romans 5:6 confirms this noting "...*at the right time Christ died for the ungodly.*" Likewise, Gal. 4:4-5 states "*But when the fullness of the time came, God sent forth His Son, born of a woman, born under the Law, so that He might redeem those who were under the Law, that we might receive the adoption as sons.*"

John 10:36 hints at some mysterious process by which the Son was prepared for His mission saying "...*Him, whom the Father sanctified and sent into the world...*"

The precise manner of the union of the human and divine nature in Christ is unrevealed to us and is beyond our comprehension. The Incarnation is thus as great of a mystery as the Trinity.

> *And the Word became flesh, and dwelt among us, and we saw His glory, glory as of the only begotten from the Father, full of grace and truth.*
> **–John 1:14**

The Incarnation was a mystery to the early church as well. The first question which Christians naturally asked was "*What do you think about the Christ?*" (Mat. 22:42).

The early church struggled with controversy and heresy that came through misunderstanding the Person of Christ. All controversy hinged on denying the reality and integrity of the two natures or the union of the two natures in Christ.

In opposition to all these errors, the correct doctrine (promulgated at Chalcedon in 451 AD) holds that in the one Person Jesus Christ there are two natures, a human nature and a divine nature. Each nature is complete and perfect. These two natures are organically and indissolubly united, so that no third nature is formed. In brief, Scripture forbids us either to divide the Person or to confound the natures.

In the following chapters, we will study both the human and divine nature of Christ and their union. Knowing Christ leads us "*to the praise of the glory of His grace, which He freely bestowed on us in the Beloved*" (Eph. 1:6).

Bible verse for devotion:

Mat. 22:42–What do you think about the Christ?

Chapter 49

The Humanity of Christ

In the Incarnation, Jesus Christ became man to live a real flesh and blood existence. He was born of a virgin. He lived, suffered, bled, died and rose again. He is the perfect man without sin.

- Jesus Christ is God made flesh.

John uses the term "flesh" (human nature) applied to Christ in John 1:14 saying *"And the Word became flesh..."* Likewise, 1 John 4:2 says *"...every spirit that confesses that Jesus Christ has come in the flesh is from God."*

Jesus called Himself, and was called, "man." In Jn. 8:40, Jesus said *"...you are seeking to kill Me, a Man who has told you the truth..."* Acts 2:22 speaks of *"...Jesus the Nazarene, a Man attested to you by God..."* 1 Cor. 15:21 teaches *"...since by a man came death, by a Man also came the resurrection of the dead."* 1 Tim. 2:5 states *"For there is one God, and one mediator also between God and men, the Man Christ Jesus."*

Jesus possessed the essential elements of human nature—a material body and a rational soul. Jesus said *"My soul is deeply grieved..."* (Mat. 26:38); *"...this is My body"* (Mat. 26:26); *"...this is My blood..."* (Mat. 26:28); *"...a spirit does not have flesh and bones as you see I have"* (Luke 24:39). Heb. 2:14 tells us that *"...since the children share in flesh and blood, He Himself likewise also partook of the same, that through death He might render powerless him who had the power of death, that is, the devil."*

Scripture shows Jesus experienced common human limitations. He knew hunger (Mat. 4:2), thirst (Jn. 19:28), weariness (Jn. 4:6), sleep (Mat. 8:24), lack of knowledge (Mk. 13:32), and sorrow (Jn. 11:33, 35). He endured temptation (Heb. 4:15). He suffered (Lk. 22:44) and died (Jn. 19:30, 34).

> *Behold, the virgin shall be with child, and shall bear a Son, and they shall call His name Immanuel, which translated means, God with us.*
> **–Matthew 1:23**

However, the virgin birth made it clear that a new thing was taking place in the earth. The One coming into the world was not simply man (Luke 1:34-35). Christ's human nature is indeed humanity perfected. Christ was born free from sin and depravity. Christ took human nature in such a way that His sinless nature bore the penalty of sin (2 Cor. 5:21).

Christ, the greatest man, shows what the true man is. The heavenly perfection of Jesus discloses to us the greatness of our own possible being, while at the same time it reveals our infinite shortcoming and the source from which all restoration must come (1 Peter 2:21-25).

Christ is not simply the noblest embodiment of the old humanity, but He is also the fountain-head and beginning of a new humanity, the new source of life for the race. This new race is created by Christ's indwelling. When Christ ascended with His perfected manhood, He sent the Holy Spirit, which is the Spirit of Christ, to make men children of God. Christ's humanity now, by virtue of its perfect union with Deity, has become universally communicable by faith. Jesus is truly "... *the root and the descendant of David...*" (Rev. 22:16).

Bible verses for devotion:

Heb. 2:17-18–Do you find comfort in His humanity?

Chapter 50

The Deity of Christ

United in Christ is both the human nature and the divine. Jesus Christ is the second Person of the Trinity. In Christ, we find all the attributes of God.

- Jesus Christ is truly God.

John 1:1 says *"In the beginning was the Word, and the Word was with God, and the Word was God."* This Scripture affirms that Christ is equal with God because He is God.

John 1:18 reads *"No one has seen God at any time; the only begotten God who is in the bosom of the Father, He has explained Him."* This ascribes absolute Deity to Christ. He is not simply the only revealer of God, but He is God revealed.

In Rom. 9:5, Paul exalts *"...Christ according to the flesh, who is over all, God blessed forever. Amen."* So too, in Titus 2:13, Paul is *"looking for the blessed hope and appearing of the glory of our great God and Savior, Christ Jesus."*

Heb. 1:8, declares *"Your throne, O God, is forever and ever..."* Heb. 1:10 follows with *"You, Lord, in the beginning laid the foundation of the earth..."* Here, these quotes are applying to Christ the Old Testament praises to Jehovah.

Ascribed to Christ are such works as the creation (Jn. 1:3; 1 Cor. 8:6; Col. 1:16), the upholding of all things (Col. 1:17; Heb. 1:3), the final raising of the dead (Jn. 5:27-29), and the judging of all men (Mat. 25:31-32). These are none other than the very works of God.

To Christ also belongs all the attributes of God. Among these are life (Jn. 1:4), self-existence (Jn. 5:26), immutability (Heb. 13:8), truth (Jn. 14:6), love (1 Jn. 3:16), holiness (Lk. 1:35), eternity (Jn. 8:58; Rev. 21:6), omnipresence (Mat. 28:20), omniscience (Col. 2:3), and omnipotence (Rev. 1:8). Christ has these attributes because, according to Colossians 2:9, *"For in Him all the fullness of Deity dwells in bodily form."*

> *And we know that the Son of God has come, and has given us understanding so that we may know Him who is true; and we are in Him who is true, in His Son Jesus Christ. This is the true God and eternal life.*
> **–1 John 5:20**

Christ possessed a knowledge of His own Deity. In John 3:13. Jesus says that He *"...has ascended into heaven."* This indicates that Christ's consciousness, at certain times in His earthly life at least, was not confined to earth. In John 14:11, Jesus says *"...I am in the Father and the Father is in Me..."*

John 5:18 states *"...the Jews were seeking all the more to kill Him, because He...was calling God His own Father, making Himself equal with God."* In Mat. 26:63-64, the high priest said to Jesus, *"I adjure You by the living God, that You tell us whether You are the Christ, the Son of God. Jesus said to him, You have said it yourself..."* Golgotha followed.

In Jn. 20:28, Thomas exclaims *"My Lord and my God!"* Unrebuked by Christ, this is a direct assertion of His Deity. Christ receives the honor and worship due to God (Acts 7:59; Rom. 10:9; Heb. 1:6; Phil. 2:10-11; Rev. 5:12-14) for Jesus is worthy. Jesus said in John 10:30 *"I and the Father are one."*

Bible verse for devotion:

Rev. 22:3–Whose throne is in heaven?

Chapter 51

The Union of Divine and Human Nature in Christ

United in Christ, the human nature and the divine are unaltered in their essence and undivested of their normal attributes and powers. With equal distinctness, these two natures represent Jesus Christ as a single undivided personality.

- Christ is properly, not God and man, but the God-man.

The human and divine natures in Christ are not bound together by the moral tie of friendship, nor by the spiritual tie which links the believer to his Lord. The two natures have a bond that is unique and inscrutable. This bond constitutes them one Person with a single will and consciousness.

Christ uniformly speaks of Himself, and is spoken of, as a single Person. There is no interchange of 'I' and 'You' between the human and the divine natures, such as we find between the Persons of the Trinity (John 17:23).

In Scripture's testimony of Christ, there is never any separation of the human from the divine, or of the divine from the human. All Christ's words were spoken, and all His deeds were done, by the one Person, the God-man.

The attributes and powers of both natures are ascribed to the one Christ. Conversely, the works and dignities of the one Christ are ascribed to two natures united in an inexplicable way, so that what each does has the value of both. The two natures are organically and permanently united in Christ.

The union of the natures was such that, although the divine nature in itself is incapable of ignorance, weakness, temptation, suffering, or death, the one Person Jesus Christ was capable of these by virtue of the union of the two natures in Him. The God-man was thus capable of absolutely infinite suffering.

> *...you were not redeemed with perishable things, like silver or gold...but with precious blood, as of a lamb unblemished and spotless, the blood of Christ. For He was foreknown before the foundation of the world, but has appeared in these last times for the sake of you.*
> **–1 Peter 1:18-20**

Scripture constantly proclaims the infinite value of Christ's atonement and the wondrous union of the human race with God through Christ. This is only intelligible when Christ is regarded, not as a man of God, but as the God-man.

The union of the divine and human in Christ makes atonement possible. 1 John 2:2 speaks of the atonement saying *"And He Himself is the propitiation for our sins; and not for ours only, but also for those of the whole world."*

This union of the divine and human in Christ makes uniting God and mankind possible. Eph. 2:16-18 says He reconciled us *"...in one body to God through the cross..."* Since Christ is man, He can make atonement for man and sympathize with man. Because Christ is God, His atonement has infinite value, and the union which He effects with God is complete. A merely human Savior could never reunite us to God. But a divine-human Savior meets all our needs.

Bible verses for devotion:

2 Pet. 1:1-4–How do we partake in the divine nature?

Chapter 52

The Humiliation of Christ

The humiliation of Christ is that act of the eternal Son by which He gave up His divine glory with the Father, in order to take a servant-form. In this act, He resigned not the possession nor the use, but rather the independent exercise, of the divine attributes.

- Christ's humiliation was a continuous self-renunciation.
- This culminated in His self-subjection to the crucifixion.

Christ laid aside His heavenly glory to be made flesh. This humiliation was voluntary to reveal the glory of God and make provision for our sins. 2 Corinthians 8:9 says *"For you know the grace of our Lord Jesus Christ, that though He was rich, yet for your sake He became poor, so that you through His poverty might become rich."*

In Christ's humiliation, omniscience gives up all knowledge but that of the child, the infant, the embryo, the infinitesimal germ of humanity. Omnipotence gives up all power but that of the impregnated ovum in the womb of the Virgin. In Christ's humiliation, the Godhead narrows itself down to a point that is next to absolute extinction.

Jesus washing His disciples' feet, in John 13:1-20, is the symbol of His coming down from His throne of glory and taking the form of a servant, in order that He may purify us, by regeneration and sanctification, for the marriage supper of the Lamb. Jesus said to Peter *"If I do not wash you, you have no part with Me."* Christ's humiliation was for us!

Christ did not give up possession of His divine attributes. To do so would be impossible as He cannot cease to be God. The attributes of the divine nature are imparted to the human without passing over into its essence. Christ, even on earth had the power to be, know, and do, as God.

> *Who, although He existed in the form of God, did not regard equality with God a thing to be grasped, but emptied Himself, taking the form of a bond-servant, and being made in the likeness of men.*
> **–Philippians 2:6-7**

That this power was latent, or was only rarely manifested, was the result of the self-chosen state of humiliation upon which the God-man had entered. In His humiliation, the communication of the contents of His divine nature to the human was mediated by the Holy Spirit.

The God-man, in His servant-form, knew and taught and performed only what the Spirit permitted and directed (Mat. 3:16; Jn. 3:34; Acts 1:2; 10:38; Heb. 9:14). When permitted, He knew, taught, and performed, not from without like the prophets, but by virtue of His own inner power (Mat. 17:2; Mk. 5:41; Luke 5:20-21; 6:19; John 2:11, 24-25; 3:13; 20:19).

Christ's humiliation culminated in His self-subjection to suffering and death for us on the cross. In Christ, the union between humanity and the deity is so close, that deity itself is brought under the curse and penalty of the law.

Since Jesus Christ was God incarnate, did He pass unscorched through the fires of Gethsemane and Calvary? Certainly not. Because Jesus Christ was God made flesh, He underwent an absolutely infinite suffering.

Bible verses for devotion:

Phil. 2:5-8–Do you have the mind of Christ?

Chapter 53

The Exaltation of Christ

The exaltation of Christ is the resumption of the eternal Son's independent exercise of divine attributes and the restoration of the glory that He shares with the Father.

- Christ's exaltation was initiated in His resurrection.
- Christ's exaltation culminated in His ascension.

In Christ's humiliation, the eternal Son of God set aside His divine glory with the Father. In Christ's exaltation, His glory with the Father is restored (Philippians 2:9-11).

Christ's exaltation includes the withdrawal of all limitations in His communication of the divine fullness to the human nature of Christ. His divine attributes are no longer obscured, but are now fully displayed.

Christ's exaltation includes the corresponding exercise, on the part of the human nature, of those powers which belonged to it by virtue of its union with the divine. Because the union of humanity with deity in the Person of Christ is indissoluble and eternal, both natures are exalted in Christ.

Christ's exaltation commenced at His resurrection. Jesus said in Jn. 10:17-18 *"For this reason the Father loves Me, because I lay down My life so that I may take it again. No one has taken it away from Me, but I lay it down on My own initiative. I have authority to lay it down, and I have authority to take it up again. This commandment I received from My Father."*

As Christ was without sin, His resurrection was a natural necessity. Acts 2:24 exalts Christ whom God raised up "...*putting an end to the agony of death, since it was impossible for Him to be held in its power.*" This meant "...*that He was neither abandoned to Hades, nor did His flesh suffer decay*" (Acts 2:31).

> *...that you will know... the working of the strength of His might which He brought about in Christ, when He raised Him from the dead and seated Him at His right hand in the heavenly places.*
> –**Ephesians 1:18-20**

The resurrection proclaimed Christ to men as the perfected and glorified man, the conqueror of sin and death.

The ascension proclaimed Christ to the universe as the reinstated God, the possessor of universal dominion, the omnipresent object of worship and hearer of prayer.

Mark 16:19 states "...*when the Lord Jesus had spoken to them, He was received up into heaven and sat down at the right hand of God.*" Eph. 1:22-23 declares "*And He put all things in subjection under His feet, and gave Him as head over all things to the church, which is His body, the fullness of Him who fills all in all.*" In Mat. 28:18, 20, Jesus said "*All authority has been given to Me in heaven and on earth... and lo, I am with you always, even to the end of the age.*"

In the ascension of Christ, glorified humanity has attained the throne of the universe. This exaltation, which then affected humanity only in its head, is to be the experience also of the members. Our bodies also are to be delivered from corruption, and we are to reign with Christ.

> **Bible verses for devotion:**
>
> **Jn. 17:1-5**–What was Christ prayer? What is yours?

Chapter 54

The Prophetic Office of Christ

A prophet is a medium of divine communication and divine revelation. He is God's mediator to man. Christ was the perfect prophet, the true revealer of God.

- Christ's prophetic work is not based on inspiration.
- Christ's prophetic work is based on incarnation.

The prophet commonly united three methods of fulfilling his office,—those of teaching, predicting, and miracle-working. In all these respects, Jesus Christ did the work of a prophet (Deut. 18:15; *cf.* Acts 3:22; Mat. 13:57; Luke 13:33; John 6:14). He taught (Mat. 5-7), He uttered predictions (Mat. 24 and 25), He wrought miracles (Mat. 8 and 9), while in His Person, His life, His work, and His death, He revealed the Father (John 8:26; 14:9; 17:8).

Christ's prophetic work began before He came in the flesh. This is evidenced in the preparatory work of the Word in enlightening mankind before the time of Christ's advent in the flesh (John 1:9). All preliminary religious knowledge, whether within or without the bounds of the chosen people, is from Christ, the revealer of God (Mat. 23:34-35).

In His earthly ministry, Christ showed Himself the prophet *par excellence.* While He submitted, like the Old Testament prophets, to the direction of the Holy Spirit, unlike them, He found the sources of all knowledge and power within Himself (Luke 6:19, Jn. 2:11). The word of God did not *come* to Him,—He was *Himself* the Word (Jn. 1:1).

Jesus was not inspired,— He was the Inspirer. Jn. 8:38, 58 says *"I speak the things which I have seen with My Father...before Abraham was born, I am."*

> **And the city has no need of the sun or of the moon to shine on it, for the glory of God has illumined it, and its lamp is the Lamb.**
> **–Revelation 21:23**

Christ's prophetic work was only begun during His earthly ministry (Acts 1:1). It is continued through the preaching of His apostles and ministers, and by the enlightening influences of the Holy Spirit (Jn. 16:12-14). The inspiration of the apostles, the illumination of all preachers and Christians to understand and to unfold the meaning of the word they wrote, the conviction of sinners, and the sanctification of believers,— all these are parts of Christ's prophetic work by the Holy Spirit.

By virtue of their union with Christ and participation in Christ's Spirit, all Christians are made in a secondary sense prophets, as well as priests and kings (Num. 11:29; Joel 2:28). All modern prophecy is true only as it is but the republication of Christ's message—the proclamation and expounding of truth already revealed in Scripture.

Christ's final revelation of the Father is to His saints in glory (John 16:25; 17:24, 26; Isa. 64:4; 1 Cor. 13:12). As the Father whom He reveals is infinite, Christ's prophetic work will be an endless one. In heaven, Christ is the visible God. We shall never see the Father *"...whom no man has seen or can see..."* apart from Christ (1 Tim. 6:16). Jn. 1:18 says *"No one has seen God at any time; the only begotten God, who is in the bosom of the Father, He has explained Him."*

Bible verse for devotion:

   1 Cor. 1:30–How did Christ become our wisdom?

Chapter 55

The Priestly Office of Christ

The priest was a person divinely appointed to transact with God on man's behalf. He fulfilled his office, first by offering sacrifice, and secondly by making intercession. In both these respects, Christ is priest.

- The priest was a mediator between God and man.

God chose the Israelites as a priestly nation, Levi as a priestly tribe, and Aaron as a priestly family. The high priest of Israel was but a type of the great High Priest, Jesus Christ.

The whole race was shut out from God by its sin. David asked in Psalm 24:3 *"Who may ascend into the hill of the Lord? And who may stand in His holy place?"* As the fundamental attribute of God is holiness, which is but self-affirming purity and right, God requires righteousness in us.

Although God's righteousness condemns sin, His love provides the remedy to sin's penalty. Scripture teaches that Christ willingly obeyed and suffered in our stead, to satisfy the demand of the divine holiness, and thus provide pardon and restoration of the guilty (Romans 5:6-11).

Christ made full propitiation for sin and satisfied the demands of holiness. His sufferings are substitutionary, since His divinity and His sinlessness enable Him to do for us what we could never do for ourselves. Christ's infinite suffering from the very hand of God is inexplicable, except as He endured the divine judgment against our sin.

What God did in condemning sin, He did through Christ. 2 Cor. 5:19 says "...*God was in Christ reconciling the world to Himself...*" He was the condemner, as well as the condemned. Christ was both the Judge and the Sin-bearer. Christ was both the High Priest and the sacrificial Lamb.

> *Therefore He is able also to save forever those who draw near to God through Him, since He always lives to make intercession for them. For it was fitting for us to have such a high priest, holy, innocent, undefiled, separated from sinners and exalted above the heavens.*
> **–Hebrews 7:25-26**

Paul distinctly declares this double work of Christ in Rom. 8:3 saying "*For what the law could not do, weak as it was through the flesh, God did: sending His own Son in the likeness of sinful flesh and as an offering for sin, He condemned sin in the flesh.*" God did through Christ what the law could not do, namely, accomplish deliverance for humanity. God did this by sending His Son in a nature which in us is identified with sin. In connection with sin, and as an offering for sin, God condemned sin, by condemning Christ.

As our High Priest, Christ also makes intercession for His people. His intercession is not just His divine petitions on our behalf. The intercession of Christ is the special activity of Christ in securing upon the ground of His sacrifice whatever blessings come to men, both temporal and spiritual.

Jesus "*...holds His priesthood permanently*" (Heb. 7:24). "*We have such a high priest, who has taken His seat at the right hand of the throne of the Majesty...*" (Heb. 8:1).

Bible verse for devotion:

Rom. 8:34–How is Christ our High Priest?

Chapter 56

The Nature of Christ's Atonement

The atonement is the satisfaction of God's demand of holiness by the substitution of Christ's penal sufferings for the punishment of the guilty.

- Punishment is the reaction of God's being against evil.
- Its demand can't be evaded, since God is forever holy.

The same God who is a God of holiness, and who in virtue of His holiness must punish human sin, is also a God of mercy, and in virtue of His mercy, He Himself bears the punishment of human sin. Christ, our High Priest, is therefore not only mediator between God and man, but also between the just God and the merciful God. In Christ, *"Lovingkindness and truth have met together; Righteousness and peace have kissed"* (Ps. 85:10).

The great classical passage with reference to the atonement is Rom. 3:25-26. It exalts Christ *"whom God displayed publicly as a propitiation (a covering) in His blood through faith. This was to demonstrate His righteousness, because in the forbearance of God He passed over the sins previously committed; for the demonstration, I say, of His righteousness at the present time, so that He would be just and the justifier of the one who has faith in Jesus."*

This passage shows that Christ's death is a propitiatory sacrifice with its first and main effect upon God. The main object of Christ's suffering is that God may be righteous while He pardons the believing sinner (Heb. 2:17, 1 Jn. 4:10).

This substitution is unknown to mere law, and above and beyond the powers of law. It is an operation of grace. Grace, however, does not violate or suspend law, but takes it up into itself and fulfills it. The righteousness of law is maintained, in that the source of all law, the judge and punisher, Himself voluntarily submits to bear the penalty.

> *He made Him who knew no sin to be sin on our behalf, so that we might become the righteousness of God in Him.*
> **–2 Cor. 5:21**

But how can Christ justly bear our penalty? In other words, how can the innocent justly suffer for the guilty?

The solution of the problem lies in Christ's union with humanity. When Christ once joined Himself to humanity, all the exposures and liabilities of humanity fell upon Him. Through Himself personally without sin, He was made sin for us. Christ inherited our guilt and our penalty.

The whole mass and weight of God's displeasure against us fell on Him, when once He became a member of the race.

As *"by Him all things were created,"* and as *"in Him all things hold together"* (Col. 1:16-17), it follows that He who is the life of humanity must, though personally pure, be involved in responsibility for all human sin, and *"that the Christ had to suffer"* (Acts 17:3). This suffering was an enduring of the reaction of the divine holiness against sin and so was a bearing of penalty (Isa. 53:6; Gal. 3:13). It was also the voluntary execution of a plan that antedated creation (Phil. 2:6-7), and Christ's sacrifice in time showed what had been in the heart of God from eternity (Heb. 9:14; Rev. 13:8).

Bible verses for devotion:

Heb. 2:14-15–What did Christ's sacrifice deliver?

Chapter 57

The Extent of Christ's Atonement

The atonement of Christ is unlimited. The whole human race might be saved through it. However, the application of the atonement is limited. Only those who repent and believe are actually saved by it.

- Scripture does not teach that all men are saved.
- The atonement is sufficient for all and effectual for many.

The Scriptures represent the atonement as having been made for all men, and as sufficient for the salvation of all. Yet, Scripture represents the atonement as limited in its application through the work of the Holy Spirit to believers.

Passages asserting that the death of Christ for all are the following: 2 Pet 2:1—"*who will secretly introduce destructive heresies, even denying the Master who bought them*"; 1 John 2:2—"*And He Himself is the propitiation for our sins; and not for ours only, but also for those of the whole world.*"; 1 Tim. 2:6—Christ Jesus "*who gave Himself a ransom for all*"; 4:10—"*the living God, who is the Savior of all men, especially of believers*"; Titus 2:11— "*For the grace of God has appeared, bringing salvation to all men.*"

Unconscious participation in the atonement of Christ, by virtue of our common humanity in Him, makes us the heirs of much temporal blessing. The atonement of Christ secures for all men a delay in the execution of the sentence against sin, and a space for repentance, together with a continuance of the common blessings of life which sin had forfeited.

Passages asserting special application of the atonement to the elect are the following: Eph. 1:4—"...*chose us in Him before the foundation of the world, that we should be holy and blameless before Him*"; Eph. 1:7—"*In Him we have redemption through His blood, the forgiveness of our trespasses, according to the riches of His grace*"; 2 Tim. 1:9-10—God "*who has saved us and called us with a holy calling, not according to our works, but according to His own purpose and grace which was granted us in Christ Jesus from all eternity, but has now been revealed by the appearing of our Savior Christ Jesus, who abolished death and brought life and immortality to light through the gospel*"; Jn. 17:9—"*I ask on their behalf; I do not ask on behalf of the world, but of those whom You have given Me...*"; Jn. 17:20—"*I do not ask on behalf of these alone, but for those also who believe in Me through their word*"; Jn. 17:24—"*Father, I desire that they also, whom You have given Me, be with Me where I am, so that they may see My glory which You have given Me...*"

> *But now apart from the Law the righteousness of God has been manifested, being witnessed by the Law and the Prophets, even the righteousness of God through faith in Jesus Christ for all those who believe...*
> **–Romans 3:21-22**

The atonement made objective provision for salvation of all by removing from the divine mind every obstacle to the pardon and restoration of sinners, except their willful opposition to God and refusal to turn to Him. Christ's Spirit overcomes this and applies the saving work of Christ to men.

Bible verse for devotion:

Luke 18:13–Have you prayed like this?

Chapter 58

The Intercession of Christ

As Christ is our High Priest, He lives to make intercession for His people. Christ's intercession is His special work in securing, upon the ground of His atoning work, every blessing that comes to men, whether that blessing be temporal or spiritual.

• Through Christ we have access to the Father.

The Priesthood of Christ does not cease with His work of atonement, but continues forever. In the presence of God, He fulfills the second office of the priest, that of intercession.

1 John 2:1 says "*...if anyone sins, we have an Advocate with the Father, Jesus Christ the righteous.*" Heb. 7:24-25 declares that Christ "*...holds His priesthood permanently...*" and "*...always lives to make intercession for them.*"

We may distinguish that general intercession which secures to all men certain temporal benefits of His atoning work, and that special intercession which secures the divine acceptance of the persons of believers and the divine bestowment of all gifts needful for their salvation.

Christ makes general intercession for all men. Isa. 53:12 prophesied "*...Yet He Himself bore the sin of many, and interceded for the transgressors.*" Luke 23:34 records "*But Jesus was saying, "Father, forgive them; for they do not know what they are doing.*" In this passage, Christ was performing His priestly intercession, even while He was being nailed to the cross.

Christ makes special intercession for His people. Luke 22:31-32 states *"Simon, Simon, behold, Satan has demanded permission to sift you like wheat; but I have prayed for you, that your faith may not fail..."* As Jesus prayed for Peter, so He prays for us in heaven.

> *Who is the one who condemns? Christ Jesus is He who died, yes, rather who was raised, who is at the right hand of God, who also intercedes for us.*
> **–Romans 8:34**

Heb. 4:15-16 encourages us that *"For we do not have a high priest who cannot sympathize with our weaknesses, but One who has been tempted in all things as we are, yet without sin. Therefore let us draw near with confidence to the throne of grace, so that we may receive mercy and find grace to help in time of need."*

Paul asks in Romans 8:32 *"He who did not spare His own Son, but delivered Him over for us all, how will He not also with Him freely give us all things?"*

The Holy Spirit is an advocate within us, teaching us how to pray as we ought. Christ is an advocate in heaven, securing from the Father the answer of our prayers. The work of Christ and of the Holy Spirit are complementary and parts of one whole (Jn. 14:26; Acts 2:33; Rom. 8:26-27).

All true intercession is either directly or indirectly the intercession of Christ. Saints on earth, by their union with Christ, the great High Priest, are themselves constituted intercessors to bear on their hearts in prayer before God the interests of family, the church, and the world (1 Tim. 2:1). Joining Christ in His work pleases our Savior (1 Tim. 2:3).

Bible verses for devotion:

1 Pet. 2:5-10–How are you a holy, royal priesthood?

Chapter 59

The Kingly Office of Christ

Christ's kingship is the sovereignty of the divine-human Redeemer. It belonged to Him of divine right from the moment of His birth, but was fully exercised only from the time of His entrance upon the state of exaltation. By virtue of this kingly office, Christ rules all things in heaven and earth, for the glory of God and the execution of God's purpose of salvation.

- As King of Kings, His glory and sovereignty are revealed.
- He is not our Prophet and Priest, unless He is our King.

The offices of Prophet, Priest, and King mutually imply one another. Christ is always a priestly Prophet and a prophetical Priest. Christ is always a royal Priest, and a priestly King. Together, they accomplish our redemption.

1 Cor. 1:30 states *"But by His doing you are in Christ Jesus, who became to us wisdom from God, and righteousness and sanctification, and redemption."* Here *"wisdom"* seems to indicate the prophetic, *"righteousness"* the priestly, and *"sanctification and redemption"* the kingly work of Christ. Christ is our Prophet to save us from the ignorance of sin. He is our Priest to save us from sin's guilt. He is our King to save us from sin's dominion in our flesh.

With respect to the universe at large, Christ's kingdom is a kingdom of power. He upholds, governs, and judges the world. The risen Christ said in Mat. 28:18 *"All authority has been given to Me in heaven and on earth."*

Hebrews 1:3 teaches that Christ "...*upholds all things by the word of His power...*" Heb. 1:8 states "*But of the Son He says: Your throne, O God, is forever and ever, and the righteousness scepter is the scepter of His kingdom.*" Christ, who was once creation's burden-bearer, is now its scepter-bearer.

> *And He is the radiance of His glory and the exact representation of His nature, and upholds all things by the word of His power. When He had made purification of sins, He sat down at the right hand of the Majesty on high.*
> **–Hebrews 1:3**

With respect to His church on earth, it is a kingdom of grace. He founds, legislates for, administers, defends, and augments His church on earth. Eph. 1:22-23 says "*And He put all things in subjection under His feet, and gave Him as head over all things to the church, which is His body, the fullness of Him who fills all in all.*" Eph. 5:25-27 displays Christ's love in that He "...*gave Himself up for her, so that He might sanctify her, having cleansed her by the washing of water with the word, that He might present to Himself the church in all her glory, having no spot or wrinkle or any such thing; but that she would be holy and blameless.*"

With respect to His church in heaven, it is a kingdom of glory. Christ rewards His redeemed people with the full revelation of Himself, upon the completion of His kingdom in the resurrection and the judgment. Jesus prayed in John 17:24, "*Father, I desire that they also, whom You have given Me, be with Me where I am, so that they may see My glory which You have given Me...*" Amen! Even so, come, Jesus!

Bible verse for devotion:

Rom. 6:14–Who has dominion over you?

VII. THE HOLY SPIRIT

Chapter 60

The Person of the Holy Spirit

The Scriptures represent the Holy Spirit as the third Person of the Triune God. He is not an impersonal force. He is a distinct from both the Father and Son.

- The Holy Spirit is not something, but Someone.

The gospels and epistles constantly represent the Holy Spirit as a Person and not an impersonal force. Acts 10:38 says *"You know of Jesus of Nazareth, how God anointed Him with the Holy Spirit and with power..."* It would be nonsensical to say God anointed Him with power and with power. Similar passages distinguishing the Holy Spirit from an impersonal power are Luke 1:35; Luke 4:14; Romans 15:13, 19 and 1 Corinthians 2:4.

1 Corinthians 12:11 says *"But one and the same Spirit works all these things, distributing to each one individually just as He wills."* In this verse, the gifts of the Spirit are traced back to the Spirit who bestows them. Here is not only giving, but giving discreetly, in the exercise of an independent will such as belongs only to a Person.

The Holy Spirit's name is mentioned in immediate connection with others, implying His own personality. He is seen in relating with Christians (Acts 15:28). He is seen in connection with Christ (Jn. 16:14). He is also described in connection with both the Father and the Son (Mat. 28:19; 2 Cor. 13:14; Jude 21; 1 Pet. 1:1-2). If the Father and the Son are Persons, the Holy Spirit must be a Person also.

The Holy Spirit manifests Himself in visible form as distinct from the Father and the Son. He does so in direct connection with personal acts performed by them.

> *The grace of the Lord Jesus Christ, and the love of God, and the fellowship of the Holy Spirit, be with you all.*
> **−2 Corinthians 13:14**

We see this manifestation evidenced in Christ's baptism as recorded in Mat. 3:16-17 and in Luke 3:21-22. Here we have a record of the prayer of Jesus, the approving voice of the Father, and the Holy Spirit descending in visible form to anoint the Son of God for His work.

The Holy Spirit performs acts that can only be ascribed to personality. That which searches, knows, speaks, testifies, reveals, convinces, commands, strives, moves, helps, guides, creates, recreates, sanctifies, inspires, makes intercession, orders the affairs of the church, performs miracles, raises the dead—cannot be a mere power, influence, efflux, or attribute of God. Such actions can only be performed by a Person (Genesis 1:2; Luke 12:12; Acts 8:29).

The Holy Spirit is affected as a Person by the acts of others. That which can be resisted (Isa. 6:10), grieved (Eph. 4:30), vexed (Acts 5:4, 9), blasphemed (Mat. 12:31-32), must be a Person. These verses reveal the mind of the Spirit, and show the infinite depths of feeling which are stirred in God's heart by the sins and needs of men. We read also of *"the love of the Spirit"* (Rom. 15:30) and unuttered sighings in intercession (Rom. 8:26-27). These deep desires are only partially revealed to us, yet prove the Holy Spirit is a Person.

Bible verses for devotion:

Rom. 8:14-17–Do you commune with the Holy Spirit? Do you hear His voice? Does He lead you?

Chapter 61

The Deity of the Holy Spirit

As spirit is nothing less than the inmost principle of life, and the spirit of man is man himself, so the Spirit of God must be God. The Holy Spirit is God Himself personally present in the believer.

• The Holy Spirit is truly God.

In Acts 5:3-4 Peter confronted Ananias who told a "*...lie to the Holy Spirit...*" Peter said "*You have not lied to men but to God.*" This Scripture affirms that the Holy Spirit is equal with God because He is God.

Paul asks in 1 Cor. 6:19 "*Or do you not know that your body is a temple of the Holy Spirit who is in you, whom you have from God, and that you are not your own?*" This verse ascribes absolute Deity to the Holy Spirit. He is the Spirit of God and demands our worship as He is worthy of it.

In 1 Peter 1:2, Peter greets the church as being chosen "*according to the foreknowledge of God the Father, by the sanctifying work of the Spirit, to obey Jesus Christ and be sprinkled with His blood: May grace and peace be yours in the fullest measure.*" Here, the church is identified with the Holy Spirit as well as God the Father and Jesus Christ.

Likewise, we see the Trinitarian formula expressed in the baptismal pronouncement of Matthew 28:19 and the apostolic benediction of 2 Corinthians 13:14. These passages give worship and honor to the Spirit of God as well as to the Father and to the Son.

Ascribed to the Holy Spirit are such works as the creation (Gen. 1:2; Job 33:4), casting out demons (Mat. 12:28), conviction of sin (Jn. 16:8), regeneration (Jn.3:8; Titus 3:5), and resurrection (Rom. 8:11; 1 Cor. 15:45). These are the works of God.

> *Do you not know that you are the temple of God and that the Spirit of God dwells in you?*
> **−1 Corinthians 3:16**

To the Holy Spirit also belongs all the attributes of God. Among these are life (Rom. 8:2), truth (Jn. 16:13), love (Rom. 5:5), holiness (Eph. 4:30), eternity (Heb. 9:14), omnipresence (Ps. 139:7), omniscience (Isa. 11:2; 1 Cor. 2:10), and omnipotence (Zech. 4:6; Luke 1:35; Rom. 15:19).

In Jn. 7:39, Jesus *"...spoke of the Spirit, whom those who believed in Him were to receive; for the Spirit was not yet given, because Jesus was not yet glorified."* Acts 2 records the giving of the Holy Spirit to the church. Yet the Bible says the Holy Spirit is *"the eternal Spirit"* (Heb. 9:14), and He not only existed, but also wrought, in Old Testament times. The Holy Spirit had been engaged in the creation and had inspired the prophets (2 Pet. 1:21). Through the working and indwelling of the Holy Spirit, God in His Person of Son was fully incarnate in Christ (Acts 10:38).

But officially, as Mediator between men and Christ, *"...the Spirit was not yet given..."* (John 7:39). The Holy Spirit could not fulfill His office as Revealer of Christ until the atoning work of Christ was accomplished. The Holy Spirit is the Spirit of Christ. The Holy Spirit is sent by both the Father and the Son, to reveal Christ, apply His perfect work to our hearts, and render the Savior forever with us.

Bible verse for devotion:

Acts 1:8–What does Holy Spirit work in us?

Chapter 62

The Work of the Holy Spirit

The Holy Spirit is the dispenser of divine grace. He applies to humanity Christ's work of redemption. He renews the ungodly and sanctifies the church.

- The Holy Spirit mediates Christ to man.

All God's revelations are through the Son or the Spirit, and the latter includes the former. As Christ is the external revelation of God, the Holy Spirit is the organ of internal revelation. The Holy Spirit takes the revelation of Christ and reveals it to the hearts of men.

1 Cor. 2:9-10 says *"But just as it is written 'Things which eye has not seen and ear has not heard, and which have not entered the heart of man, all that God has prepared for those who love Him.' For to us God revealed them through the Spirit; for the Spirit searches all things, even the depths of God."* Only the Holy Spirit can give us an inward apprehension or realization of the truth. Only the Holy Spirit can apply Christ's saving work to our hearts (1 Cor. 6:11).

The Spirit's work is conviction, revelation, quickening and conversion in the sinner. In Jn. 16:8, Jesus said *"And He, when He comes, will convict the world concerning sin and righteousness and judgment."* It is the Holy Spirit that quickens the sinner. God said in Eze. 37:14 *"I will put My Spirit within you, and you come to life..."* Jesus said to enter His kingdom, you must be *"...born of the Spirit"* (Jn. 3:3-8). The Holy Spirit is the principle of all movement toward God.

It is through the Holy Spirit that Christ offered Himself without blemish unto God (Heb. 9:14). So too, it is only through the Holy Spirit that fallen man can return to God and that the church has access to the Father (Eph. 2:18).

> *But when the fullness of the time came, God sent forth His Son, born of a woman, born under the Law, so that He might redeem those who were under the Law, that we might receive the adoption as sons. Because you are sons, God has sent forth the Spirit of His Son into our hearts, crying, Abba! Father!*
> **–Galatians 4:4-6**

The Spirit not only enlightens the sinner, but also the saint. He is the Spirit of revelation and sanctification in us. Jn. 16:13 says "*...when He, the Spirit of truth, comes, He will guide you into all the truth...*" Rom. 8:14 declares "*For all who are being led by the Spirit of God, these are sons of God.*"

He is also the Spirit of power, consolation, and witness to the saint. Jesus said in John 14:16 "*I will ask the Father, and He will give you another Helper, that He may be with you forever.*" He teaches us how to pray and intercedes for us (Rom. 8:26). As Christ is our Advocate before the throne, the Holy Spirit is the Advocate in our own heart. Rom. 8:16 states "*The Spirit Himself testifies with our spirit that we are children of God.*"

The Holy Spirit completes the Trinity. Likewise, the office of the Holy Spirit is that of concluding, completing, and perfecting. Thus, the work of the Holy Spirit is the application of the work of Christ.

Bible verse for devotion:

Jn. 14:18–How does Christ come to us?

VIII. THE REDEMPTIVE WORK OF CHRIST APPLIED BY THE HOLY SPIRIT

Chapter 63

Election

> *Election is the eternal act of God by which in His sovereign pleasure and on account of no foreseen merit in them, He chooses some sinful men to be the recipients of the special grace of His Spirit and so to be made voluntary partakers of Christ's salvation.*

- Election makes certain that Christ's death is not in vain.

Election is a doctrine taught with reverent humility throughout Scripture. In Eph. 1:4-5, Paul writes *"just as He chose us in Him before the foundation of the world, that we would be holy and blameless before Him in love. He predestined us to adoption as sons through Jesus Christ to Himself, according to the kind intention of His will."*

The doctrine of election is only a special application of the doctrine of decrees. God's decrees are certain from eternity. They are not of possible events, but of what is to be. They are the eternal act of an infinitely perfect will, framed by His wisdom and goodness. The decrees never conflict with man's free will. They are not addressed to men and are only revealed after they occur. All of this is also true of election.

Election is not based on man's foreseen faith. Depravity of the human will is such that, without election, all would reject Him. Election proceeds rather upon foreseen unbelief. Faith itself is God's gift. Thus, its initiative must be wholly with God. Election turns on who gets the credit in initiating salvation (Jn. 1:13). It exalts God's preeminence over man.

Election deals with men who are guilty and condemned. That any should be saved, is matter of pure grace. Those who are not included in this purpose of salvation suffer only the due reward of their deeds. There is no injustice in God's election (Rom. 9:14-16).

> *...God has chosen you from the beginning for salvation through sanctification by the Spirit and faith in the truth.*
> **−2 Thes. 2:13**

It is not a decree to destroy; it is only to save. We may better praise God that He saves any, than charge Him with injustice because He saves so few.

No man can be saved without God. But it is also true that there is no man whom God is not willing to save. Nothing prevents a man's pardon but his own unwillingness to accept God's pardon. God's decree is as absolute as if there were no freedom, yet it leaves man as free as if there were no decree.

We must remember that God's sovereignty is the sovereignty of God — the infinitely wise, holy and loving God. God can say to all men, saved or unsaved, *"Friend, I am doing you no wrong...Is it not lawful for me to do what I wish with what is my own?"* (Mat. 20:13, 15).

God does not elect to save any without repentance and faith. Some hold the doctrine of election, but the doctrine does not hold them. Such should ponder 1 Peter 1:2, where Christians are said to be elect *"...by the sanctifying work of the Spirit, to obey Jesus Christ and be sprinkled with His blood..."* Election comforts and humbles believers. Ps. 115:1 says *"Not to us, O LORD, not to us, but to Your name give glory because of Your lovingkindess, because of Your truth."*

Bible verses for devotion:

Mat. 11:27-28; Jn. 6:37–Ponder election and gospel.

Chapter 64

Calling

Calling is that act of God by which men are invited to accept, by faith, the salvation provided by Christ. The Scriptures distinguish between the general or external call to all men through God's providence, word and Spirit and the special or internal call to God's elect.

- The inward call of the Spirit is effectual.

God's invitation to receive salvation goes out to all men. Isaiah 45:22 declares *"Turn to Me, and be saved, all the ends of the earth; For I am God, and there is no other."* Eze. 33:11 pleads *"...As I live declares the LORD God, I take no pleasure in the death of the wicked, but rather that the wicked turn from his way and live. Turn back, turn back from your evil ways! Why then will you die, O house of Israel?"*

God's gospel call to all men is sincere despite the moral inability found in the perversity of man's evil will. God's call is no less sincere than His command to love Him perfectly. One may be perfectly sincere in giving an invitation which he knows will be refused. 1 Tim. 2:4 declares God *"...desires all men to be saved and to come to the knowledge of the truth."*

Scripture describes an inward call of Christ by which the Spirit takes the outward call of the gospel and applies it to His elect. 1 Cor. 1:23-24 says *"but we preach Christ crucified, to Jews a stumbling block and to Greeks foolishness, but to those who are called, both Jews and Greeks, Christ the power of God and the wisdom of God."*

The Spirit's inward call creates in man a new disposition of the heart and a new activity of the will, by which the sinner accepts Christ. It is not a man reviving his own will nor is it mere cooperation with the will of God. It is an almighty act of God in the will of man by which its freedom to choose God as its end is restored and rightly exercised (Rom. 8:28-30).

> *Who has saved us and called us with a holy calling, not according to our works, but according to His own purpose and grace which was granted us in Christ Jesus from all eternity.*
> **−2 Timothy 1:9**

This inward call originates in God for His own glory. In 2 Thes. 2:13-14, Paul states "*...God has chosen you from the beginning for salvation through sanctification by the Spirit and faith in the truth. It was for this He called you through our gospel, that you may gain the glory of our Lord Jesus Christ.*"

The Spirit's inward call infallibly accomplishes its end of leading the sinner to the acceptance of salvation. His saving grace and effectual calling are resistible, but they are never successfully resisted. Some use the term 'irresistible grace', but this implies a coercion and compulsion that is foreign to the very nature of God's working in the soul (Psalm 110:3).

The only obstacle to the gospel on the sinner's part is the sinner's own evil will. God has made, at an infinite cost, a complete external provision upon which "*one who wishes*" may "*come*" and "*take the water of life without cost*" (Rev. 22:17). God can truly say: "*What more was there to do for My vineyard that I have not done in it?*" (Isa. 5:4).

Bible verses for devotion:

Phil. 2:12-13–How is our work God's work?

Chapter 65

Union with Christ

Union is that act of God by which men are united with Christ. Man, while maintaining his own individuality and personal distinctness, is interpenetrated and energized by the Spirit of Christ. Man is therefore made inexplicably yet indestructibly one with a personal, risen, living, omnipresent Lord.

- Christ doesn't dwell outside His people, but within them.

Christ's union with humanity at the incarnation enabled Him to assume the penalty of our sin and fully satisfy God's divine justice. Jesus thus removed all external obstacles to man's return to God. An internal obstacle, however, still remains — the evil affections and will, and the consequent guilt, of the individual soul. This last obstacle Christ also removes by uniting Himself to His people by His Spirit.

Scripture says that the believer is indeed *"in Christ"* (Rom. 6:11; Rom. 8:1; 2 Cor. 5:17; Eph. 2:13). The fact that the believer is in Christ, is symbolized in baptism — we are *"baptized into Christ"* (Gal. 3:27). Likewise, to the believer, Scripture teaches that Christ is *"in you"* (Jn. 14:20, 23; Rom. 8:9-10). This is symbolized in the Lord's Supper. 1 Cor. 10:16 asks *"Is not the cup...a sharing in the blood of Christ? Is not the bread...a sharing in the body of Christ?"*

Scripture teaches that the believer only has life by union with Christ. Jesus said that without Him, *"you have no life in you"* (Jn. 6:53-58). In Christ is life in abundance (Jn. 10:10).

Scripture teaches that our union with Christ makes all believers collectively united in Christ (Jn. 17:21-23). A believer *"joins himself to the Lord is one spirit with Him"* (1 Cor. 6:17), and together, we become *"partakers*

> *In that day you will know that I am in My Father, and you in Me, and I in you.*
> **–John 14:20**

of the divine nature" (2 Pet. 1:4). Just as the Son of God receives the Spirit without measure, so too believers in like manner receive Christ.

Union with Christ is fundamental in the New Testament. It is illustrated by the union of a building and its foundation (Eph. 2:20-22; 1 Pet. 2:4-5), by the union of a husband and a wife (Rom. 7:4; Eph. 5:31-32; Rev. 19:7), and by the union of the vine and its branches (Jn. 15:1-10). It is also illustrated by the union between the members and the head of the body (1 Cor. 6:15, 19; Eph. 1:22-23), and from the union of the race with Adam (Rom. 5:12, 21; 1 Cor. 15:22, 45, 49).

Union with Christ results in common sonship, relation to God, character, influence and destiny. Scripture teaches that we are crucified together with Christ (Gal. 2:20). We died together with Christ (Col. 2:20). We are buried together with Christ (Rom. 6:4). We are quickened together with Christ (Eph. 2:5). We are raised together with Christ (Col. 3:1). As joint heirs with Christ and fellow sufferers with Christ, we will also be glorified together with Him (Rom. 8:17).

Christ does not work upon believers from without, as one separated from us, but from within. Col. 3:3 states *"For you died and your life is hidden with Christ in God."* Gal. 2:20 says *"...it is no longer I who live, but Christ lives in me..."* He is the very heart from which the life-blood of our spirit flows.

Bible verse for devotion:

Col. 1:24-29–Does union with Christ animate you?

Chapter 66

Regeneration

Regeneration is that act of God by which the governing disposition of the soul is made holy and its first holy exercise is secured by the Holy Spirit.

- Regeneration is the Holy Spirit turning the soul to God.
- Union with Christ and Regeneration are simultaneous.

To have fellowship with a holy God, a radical internal change is requisite in every human soul. It is a change which constitutes its entire character. Man's natural tendencies are wholly in the direction of selfishness (Jer. 13:23). A reversal of his inmost dispositions and principles of action is needed if he is to set his love supremely upon God (Eze. 11:19).

Regeneration is the direct operation of the Holy Spirit upon the sinner's heart which changes its moral character.

There are two aspects of regeneration. In the first, the soul is passive as the Holy Spirit changes man's governing disposition. In this change the soul is simply acted upon. In the second, the Holy Spirit secures the initial exercise of this disposition in view of the truth. In this, the soul itself acts.

These two operations are simultaneous. As God renews mans' soul, He pours in the light of His truth and induces the exercise of the holy disposition He has imparted (Acts 16:14).

This distinction between the passive and the active aspects of regeneration is necessitated by the twofold method of representing this change in Scripture.

In many passages, the change is ascribed wholly to the power of God (Eph. 2:1). The soul is radically changed. In other passages, there is an appeal to man's rational nature through truth (Ja. 1:18). The Holy Spirit presents truth, and the mind acts in its light.

> *Truly, truly, I say to you, unless one is born again, he cannot see the kingdom of God.*
> **–John 3:3**

The distinction between the two aspects of regeneration seems to be intimated in Ephesians 2:5-6 — *"made us alive together with Christ"* and *"raised us up with Him."* Lazarus was first made alive. In this, he could not cooperate. But he also came forth from the tomb. In this, he did act (Jn. 11:44).

In regeneration, sinful nature is not gone, but its power is broken. Sin no longer dominates the life (Rom. 6:18). Sin has been thrust from the center to the circumference. It has the sentence of death in itself. Regenerate man is freed, at least in potency and promise. He will yet be sanctified.

Regeneration, or the new birth, is the divine side of that change of heart which we call conversion if viewed from the human side. Regeneration is God's turning the soul to Him, while conversion is the soul's turning itself to God. God's turning the soul is both the accompaniment and cause as man turns only as God turns him (Jn. 6:44; 65; 1 Cor. 3:6-7).

Yet, the necessity of regeneration implies its possibility. In Jn. 3:7, Jesus said *"You must be born again."* This equals "You may be born again". This verse is not merely a warning and a command, it is also a promise. Every sinner has the chance of making a new start in Christ (2 Cor. 5:17).

[handwritten margin note: We are still sinners, but with Christ. Sin no longer has a hold of us. "He who is in us is greater than he who is in the world." –1 John 4:4]

Bible verse for devotion:

   1 Cor. 2:2–What must we manifest to every man?

Chapter 67

Conversion

Conversion is that voluntary change in the mind of the sinner, in which he turns, on the one hand, from sin, and on the other hand, to Christ.

- In Conversion, the turning from sin is called repentance.
- In Conversion, the turning to Christ is called faith.

Conversion is the human side or aspect of that fundamental spiritual change which, when viewed from the divine side, we call regeneration. It is simply man's turning. Scripture recognizes the voluntary activity of the human soul in this change as distinctly as it recognizes God's causation.

While God turns men to Himself (Ps. 85:4; Song. 1:4; Jer. 31:18; Lam. 5:21), men are exhorted to turn themselves to God (Pr. 1:23; Isa. 31:6; 59:20; Eze. 14:6; 18:32; 33:9, 11; Joel 2:12-14). While God is represented as the author of the new heart and the new spirit (Ps. 51:10; Eze. 11:19; 36:26), men are commanded to make for themselves a new heart and spirit (Eze. 18:31; 2 Cor. 7:1; Phil. 2:12, 13; Eph. 5:14).

This twofold depiction is only explained by remembering that man's powers may be interpenetrated and quickened by the divine, not only without destroying man's freedom, but with the result of making man for the first time truly free.

The relation between the divine and the human activity is not one of chronological succession. Man is never to wait for God's working. If a sinner is ever regenerated, he turns to God unconstrained. Man's action accompanies God's action.

Whenever the Holy Spirit works in regeneration, there is always accompanying it a voluntary change in man. This change is what we call conversion. This change is as free and as really man's own work, as if there were no divine influence upon him.

> *And the hand of the Lord was with them, and a large number who believed turned to the Lord.*
> –Acts 11:21

Conversion is like the invasion of a kingdom. Mat. 11:12 says "*...the kingdom of heaven suffers violence, and violent men take it by force.*" Men are not to wait for God, but to act at once with impassioned earnestness of soul. "*Work out your salvation*" in Paul's exhortation comes before "*for it is God who is at work in you*" (Phil. 2:12-13). This means that our first business is to use our wills in obedience. We will then find that God has gone before us to prepare us to obey.

Conversion involves repentance. Repentance is that voluntary change in the mind of the sinner in which he turns from sin. It is abandonment of sin rather than just sorrow for it (Ps. 51:5, 7, 10; Jer. 25:5). Repentance takes God's part against ours, has sympathy with God, and is grieved how the Ruler, Father, and Friend of men is treated (Rom. 2:4).

Conversion involves faith. Faith is that voluntary change in the mind of the sinner in which he turns to Christ as Lord and Savior. By faith, the soul surrenders itself, as guilty and defiled, to Christ's governance as Lord (Mat. 11:28-29, Jn. 8:12). By faith, the soul receives and appropriates Christ for pardon and spiritual life (Acts 16:31; Jn. 20:31). Faith is not simple receptiveness. It gives itself as well as receives Christ. Faith and repentance are different sides of the same turning.

Bible verses for devotion:

John 6:35-40–Have you come to Jesus?

Chapter 68

Justification

> *Justification is that judicial act of God by which, on account of Christ, to whom the sinner is united by faith, He declares that sinner to be no longer exposed to the penalty of the law but to be restored to favor.*

- In Justification, there is remission of punishment.
- In Justification, there is restoration of favor.

The moment of our union with Christ is also the moment we are regenerated and justified. The communion of benefits which results from this union involves a change of state or relation which is called justification (Col. 3:3; Rom. 3:24-26).

Justification is the reversal of God's attitude toward the sinner because of the sinner's new relation to Christ. God did condemn; He now acquits. He did repel; He now gives favor.

The only condition of justification is the sinner's faith in Jesus, which merges the life of the sinner in the life of Christ.

In Gal. 2:16, the apostle Paul teaches "....*a man is not justified by the works of the Law but through faith in Jesus Christ...*" Paul's teaching finds support in the Old Testament. Rom. 4:5-8 says "*But to him who does not work, but believes on Him who justifies the ungodly, his faith is accounted for righteousness, just as David also describes the blessedness of the man to whom God imputes righteousness apart from works: Blessed are those whose lawless deeds are forgiven, and whose sins have been covered. Blessed is the man whose sin the LORD will not take into account.*"

The usage of the epistle of James does not contradict this. The doctrine of James is that we are justified only by such faith as makes us faithful and brings forth good works (James 2:14-26). James doesn't deny salvation to him who has faith, but only to him who falsely professes to have it. James is denouncing a dead faith, while Paul speaks of the necessity of a living faith.

> *Now that no one is justified by the Law before God is evident; for the righteous man shall live by faith.*
> **–Galatians 3:11**

In justification, God acquits the ungodly who believe in Christ, and declares them to be just. This is based solely in the bearing of penalty by Christ, to whom the sinner is united by faith. The demands of the law have been satisfied and they are now free from its condemnation (Rom. 8:1-2).

In justification, God treats the sinner as if he were, and had been, personally righteous. This is based solely in the perfect obedience of Christ, to whom the sinner is united by faith. On account of Christ, our relation to God is restored in friendship (James 2:23) and adoption (Jn. 1:12; Gal. 4:4-7).

Remission is never separated from restoration. Failure to apprehend this favor is the reason why so many Christians have little joy and enthusiasm in their religious lives. The preaching of the magnanimity and generosity of God makes the gospel "... *the power of God to salvation...*" (Rom. 1:16).

Forgiveness seems easy to us, largely because we are indifferent toward sin. But to the Holy One who abhors sin, forgiveness involves a fundamental change of relation. This is possible only by Christ's bearing the penalty of our sins.

Bible verses for devotion:

Rom. 5:1-2–Do you stand forever in God's favor?

"Therefore, since we have been justified through faith, we have peace with God through our Lord Jesus Christ, through whom we have gained access by faith into this grace in which we now stand. And we boast in the hope of the glory of God."

Chapter 69

Sanctification

Sanctification is that continuous operation of the Holy Spirit, by which the holy disposition imparted in regeneration is maintained and strengthened.

- Sanctification is a continual process through our lifetime.
- It is the work of the Holy Spirit to make us like Christ.

The moment of our union with Christ is also the moment our sanctification begins. The communion of benefits, which results from this union, involves a change of subjective moral character. This change is commenced in regeneration and completed throughout our life by sanctification (Phil. 1:6).

In justification, the right relationship between God and man is restored. In sanctification, the fruit of this renewed order is secured. God declares the sinner righteous in order that He may restore him to holiness. A broken ship is brought into port and secured to the dock. She is safe, but not sound. Repairs may take a long time. Christ makes us safe by justification and sound through sanctification.

In Phil. 3:12-14, Paul testifies *"Not that I have already obtained it or have already become perfect, but I press on so that I may lay hold of that for which also I was laid hold of by Christ Jesus. Brethren, I do not regard myself as having laid hold of it yet; but one thing I do: forgetting what lies behind and reaching forward to what lies ahead, I press on toward the goal for the prize of the upward call of God in Christ Jesus."*

Redemption is indeed past, present and future. Justification is a past fact, sanctification is a present process and resurrection and glory are a future consummation (1 Jn. 3:2).

In regeneration, our governing disposition is made holy. Yet, we still contend with tendencies to evil which lasts throughout life (Rom. 7; Gal. 5:17). In Christ, we have both

> *Now may the God of peace Himself sanctify you entirely; and may your spirit and soul and body be preserved complete, without blame at the coming of our Lord Jesus Christ. Faithful is He who calls you, and He also will bring it to pass.*
> **–1 Thes. 5:23-24**

deliverance from sin's penalty and the promise of new life that conquers sin. Christ sanctifies us (Col. 1:21-22) by His word (Jn. 17:17).

The vinedresser ensures that the vine bears fruit. Dead wood is cut out and living wood must be cut back (Jn. 15:2). Sanctification requires a divine superintendence and surgery on the one hand and, on the other hand, a practical hatred of evil on our part that cooperates with the husbandry of God.

The Holy Spirit enables the believer to more fully and consciously appropriate Christ by increasing faith, and thus progressively conquer the remaining sinfulness of his nature (Rom. 8:13-14). As we get air out of a vessel by pouring in water, so we drive out sin by bringing in Christ (Rom. 13:14).

Our sanctification is certain. 2 Cor. 3:18 promises us that "... *we all, with unveiled face, beholding as in a mirror the glory of the Lord, are being transformed into the same image from glory to glory, just as from the Lord, the Spirit.*"

Bible verses for devotion:

Jude 24-25–Is God able to present you faultless?

Chapter 70

Perseverance

Perseverance is voluntary continuance in faith on the part of the Christian. It is the certitude that all who are united to Christ by faith will infallibly continue in a state of grace and will finally attain to everlasting life.

* Perseverance is to take hold, hold on, and never let go.
* The Holy Spirit works in us so that we freely persevere.

Perseverance is the human side or aspect of that spiritual process which, when viewed from the divine side, we call sanctification. It is not a mere natural consequence of conversion. It involves a constant activity of the human will from the moment of conversion to the end of our earthly life.

The only falling from grace described in Scripture is the falling of the unregenerate from influences pointing them to Christ, not the falling of the regenerate. God has graciously decreed to give believers the kingdom (Luke 12:32). Yet this keeping by God, which we call sanctification, is accompanied and followed by a keeping of himself on the part of the believer. This keeping of self is perseverance (1 Cor. 9:27).

Sanctification is alluded to in Jn. 17:11 where Jesus prays "...*Holy Father, keep them in Your name, the name which You have given Me...*" Perseverance is alluded to in 1 Tim. 5:22 where Paul writes "...*keep yourself free from sin.*" Jude 21, 24 teaches us both to "*keep yourselves in the love of God...*" and to praise "...*Him who is able to keep you from stumbling...*" God upholds us and we hold on to Him.

Every believer is required to continuously and fervently surrender himself to divine action. 2 Peter 1:10-11 says "...*be all the more diligent to make certain about His calling and choosing you; for as long as you practice these things, you will never stumble; for in this way the entrance into the eternal kingdom of our Lord and Savior Jesus Christ will be abundantly supplied to you.*"

> *My sheep hear My voice, and I know them, and they follow Me; and I give eternal life to them, and they will never perish; and no one will snatch them out of My hand. My Father, who has given them to Me, is greater than all; and no one is able to snatch them out of the Father's hand.*
> **–John 10:27-29**

2 Tim. 2:19 teaches "*Nevertheless the firm foundation of God stands, having this seal: The Lord knows those who are His, and, Everyone who names the name of the Lord is to abstain from wickedness.*" Christian character thus has on its foundation two significant inscriptions, the one declaring God's power, wisdom and purpose of salvation; the other the purity of holy activity on the part of the believer in which Christ's purpose will certainly be fulfilled (1 Pet. 1:2, 5).

In 2 Tim. 1:13-14, Paul says "*Retain the standard of sound words which you have heard from me, in the faith and love which are in Christ Jesus. Guard, through the Holy Spirit who dwells in us, the treasure which has been entrusted to you.*" Paul confidently prefaces this with "*...I know whom I have believed and I am convinced that He is able to guard what I have entrusted to Him until that day.*"

Bible verses for devotion:

1 Cor. 10:12-13–Consider God's faithfulness.

IX. THE CHURCH

Chapter 71

The Definition of the Church

The church of Christ is the whole company of regenerate persons in all times and ages, in heaven and on earth. The church is redeemed humanity in which God in Christ exercises spiritual dominion.

- The church is a spiritual body of only the regenerate.
- The church is indwelt by the Holy Spirit for God's glory.

The church is the great company of persons whom Christ has saved, in whom He dwells, to whom and through whom He reveals God. In Gen. 15:5, God said to Abraham *"Now look toward the heavens, and count the stars, if you are able to count them...So shall your descendants be."* The church is the fulfillment of this promise. It includes all true believers.

Union with Christ is the presupposition of the church. This alone transforms the sinner into a Christian. This alone makes possible that vital and spiritual fellowship between individuals which constitutes the church. The same divine life which ensures the pardon and the perseverance of the believer unites him to all other believers (1 Cor. 12:13-14).

The church is nothing less than the body of Christ. The church is a supernatural body manifesting the very glory of God. It is the organism to which God gives spiritual life, and through which He shows the fullness of His power and grace. Eph. 1:22-23 says *"And He put all things in subjection under His feet, and gave Him as head over all things to the church, which is His body, the fullness of Him who fills all in all."*

The church cannot be defined in merely human terms, as a group of individuals united for social, benevolent, or even spiritual purposes.

> *He is also head of the body, the church; and He is the beginning, the firstborn from the dead, so that He Himself will come to have first place in everything.*
> **–Colossians 1:18**

The indwelling Christ makes the church superior to and more permanent than all humanitarian organizations; they die, but because Christ lives, the church lives. The church is immortal, since it draws its life from Christ (Isa. 65:22; Zech. 4:2-3). God has truly "...*raised us up with Him, and seated us with Him in the heavenly places in Christ Jesus*" (Eph. 2:6).

James 1:18 says "*In the exercise of His will He brought us forth by the word of truth, so that we would be a kind of first fruits among His creatures.*" Believers are "*first fruits*" because from them blessing will spread until the whole world will be pervaded with new life. We are saved not for us only, but as parts and beginnings of God's kingdom (Luke 13:19).

In Acts 1:8, Jesus said "...*you shall be My witnesses both in Jerusalem, and in all Judea and Samaria, and even to the remotest part of the earth.*" As God can be seen only through Christ, so the Holy Spirit can be seen only through the church. As Christ is the image of the invisible God, so the church is appointed to be the image of the invisible Christ.

As we are united in Christ, "*Now all things are from God, who reconciled us to Himself through Christ, and gave us the ministry of reconciliation*" (2 Cor. 5:18).

Bible verses for devotion:

Eph. 2:18-22– How is the church God's temple?

Chapter 72

The Organization of the Church

The organization of the local church exists in regenerate members united in equality with one another and independence from other churches. Their sole authority is the will of Christ as expressed in Scripture. Their only object is the glory of God.

- The church is distinguished from unregenerate humanity.
- The early church's association resulted in organization.

Scripture bears witness to formal organization in the church. It is shown from its stated meetings (Acts 20:7, Heb. 10:25), elections (Acts 1:23-26; 6:5-6), and officers (Phil. 1:1). It is shown by designations of its ministers (Acts 20:17, 28), together with the recognized authority of the minister and of the church (Mat. 18:17; 1 Pet. 5:2). It is shown in discipline (1 Cor. 5:4-5, 13), contributions (Rom. 15:26; 1 Cor. 16:1-2), letters of commendation (Acts 18:27; 2 Cor. 3:1), registers of widows (1 Tim. 5:9; Acts 6:1), uniform customs (1 Cor. 11:16), and ordinances (Acts 2:41; 1 Cor. 11:23-26). It is shown by order enjoined and observed (1 Cor. 14:40; Col. 2:5), the qualifications for membership (Mat. 28:19; Acts 2:47), and the common work of the whole body (Phil. 2:30).

As each member bears supreme allegiance to Christ, the church as a body must recognize Christ as the only lawgiver. All believers have the Spirit of Christ dwelling in them. 1 Jn. 2:20 says *"But you have an anointing from the Holy One, and you all know."* A church's relation to a believer must only further his relation to Christ, never supersede it.

As each regenerate man recognizes every other as a brother in Christ, individual members are upon a footing of absolute equality (Mat. 23:8-10). In Jn. 15:5, Jesus said *"I am the vine, you are the branches..."* No one branch of the vine outranks another. One

> *And all the more believers in the Lord, multitudes of men and women, were constantly added to their number.*
> *—Acts 5:14*

may be more advantageously situated, more ample in size, or more fruitful. But all are alike in kind. All draw their vitality from one source, Jesus Christ. There can be no rightful human lordship over God's heritage (1 Pet. 5:3).

As a local church is directly subject to Christ, there is no jurisdiction of one church over another. All are on an equal footing. Just as each believer has personal dealings with Christ and for even the pastor to come between him and his Lord is treachery to Christ, so too is any attempt to subject one church to another or to a group of churches (Rom. 14:4). Likewise, churches must also be independent of interference or control by a civil power (Mat. 22:21; Acts 5:29; Ezra 8:22).

The sole object of the local church is the glory of God, in the complete establishment of His kingdom, both in the hearts of believers and in the world. This objective involves united worship, including prayer and religious instruction (Heb. 10:25). It includes mutual watchcare and exhortation (1 Thes. 5:11; Heb. 3:13). It must entail common labors for the reclamation of the impenitent world (Acts 8:4; Jude 23). Local churches exists for us to *"...consider how to stimulate one another to love and good deeds"* (Heb. 10:24). The light that shines the furthest shines brightest nearest home.

Bible verses for devotion:

Mat. 16:18; Acts 2:47– Who builds the church?

Chapter 73

Government of the Church

Christ is the sole authority and lawgiver in His Church. In determining the will of Christ and in applying His commands, the Holy Spirit guides the whole body to right conclusions. God has appointed the offices of Elder and Deacon to minister to and serve the church.

- Christ alone rules His church.
- His will is obeyed by the church in the unity of the Spirit.

Christ is the authority of the church. While Christ is sole king, the government of the church resembles a democracy in the interpretation and execution of His will by the body.

The whole church is entrusted with the shared duty and responsibility of carrying out the laws of Christ as expressed in His word. This is necessary to be the "...*church of the living God, the pillar and support of the truth*" (1 Tim. 3:15).

As the representative and guardian of God's truth, the church must be rightly governed by the Holy Spirit working in and through it. The Holy Spirit enlightens one member through the counsel of another. The result is a combined deliberation, by which the whole body is led to right decision.

It is this very relation of the church to Christ and His truth which renders it needful to insist upon the right of each member of the church to his private judgment as to the meaning of Scripture. No majority can bind him against his conviction of duty to Christ. Likewise, each member, as equal to every other, has right to a voice in the church's decisions.

This unity is only possible by yielding to the Spirit (Eph. 4:1-6). The whole church must strive for this unity (1 Cor. 1:10). Unity by the inflowing of Christ's Spirit is better than any external unity, whether of organization or creed.

It is the responsibility of the entire church to maintain a pure faith and practice. In Rev. 2 and 3, Christ exhorts the seven churches of Asia to good doctrine and works. These letters are directly addressed to the entire church. It is for each and every member to obey.

> *Only conduct yourselves in a manner worthy of the gospel of Christ, so that whether I come and see you or remain absent, I will hear of you that you are standing firm in one spirit, with one mind striving together for the faith of the gospel.*
> **–Philippians 1:27**

To help the church keep its faith and witness, two offices are recognized in the church. The first is the office of elder. It is sometimes referred to as "bishop" or "pastor" (Acts 20:28; Phil. 1:1; 1 Tim. 3:1; Titus 1:5, 7; 1 Pet. 5:1-3). The role of the elder is primarily to shepherd and teach (Acts 20:18-35).

The second office recognized in the church is that of deacon. The deacon is a helper to the elders and the church in both spiritual and temporal things. He relieves the pastors of external labors and helps in tending the flock (Acts 6:1-7).

Qualifications of deacons and elders are found in Titus 1:5-9 and 1 Timothy 3:1-13. Elders and deacons are priests only as every Christian is a priest (Rev. 1:6). Elders and deacons are but humble stewards of the church. The Spirit of Christ is the true Administrator of His Church.

Bible verses for devotion:

1 Tim. 5:17-19– How do you honor your ministers?

Chapter 74

The Relation of Local Churches to One Another

Local churches relate to one another as fellowship between equals. As they are one in Christ, churches should share in consultation and cooperation.

- Churches can help one another in advice and counsel.
- Churches can help one another in advancing the Gospel.

No church or council of churches, nor association or convention, can relieve any single church of its direct responsibility to Christ. The New Testament never presents an authority on earth above that of the local church.

However, no church can properly ignore, or disregard, the existence or work of other churches around it. Every other church is presumptively possessed of the Spirit, in equal measure with itself. There must be sympathy and mutual furtherance of each other's welfare among churches.

This fellowship involves the duty of special consultation with regard to matters affecting the common interest. This duty includes both seeking advice and giving advice. Since the order and good reputation of each is valuable to all the others, cases of grave importance and difficulty in internal discipline can be submitted to an association for counsel.

Such admonition or advice, whether coming from a single church or a group, is not itself of binding authority. It is simply in the nature of moral persuasion. The receiving church must still compare it with Christ's laws. Ultimate decisions rest with the church so advised or asking advice.

The relation of churches to one another is analogous to the relation of private Christians to one another. Never is a meddlesome spirit is to be allowed. But in matters of grave moment, a church, as well as an individual, may be offered advice unasked.

> *There is neither Jew nor Greek, there is neither slave nor free man, there is neither male nor female; for you are all one in Christ Jesus.*
> **–Galatians 3:28**

Independence is qualified by interdependence. While each church bears its own responsibility in ascertaining doctrine and duty, it is to acknowledge the indwelling of the Holy Spirit in other churches as well. It must value the public opinion of churches as an indication of the mind of Christ.

The church in Antioch asked advice of the church in Jerusalem, although Paul himself was at Antioch (Acts 15:2). While no church or union has jurisdiction over a single body, their counsel should be regarded as an index to truth. Only grave reasons will justify a church in ignoring or refusing it.

The principle of church independence is consistent with cooperation with other churches. Each church should recall that, though it is honored by the indwelling of Christ, it is only a part of that great body of which He is head (Col. 1:18).

Cooperation in mission work (3 Jn. 1:8), giving (2 Cor. 8:16-24), evangelical enterprises (Mark 2:3), and Biblical education (2 Tim. 3:16-17) are natural outgrowths of this principle. In John 17:23, Jesus prayed for believers to *"...be perfected in unity, so that the world may know that You sent Me, and loved them, even as You have loved Me."*

Bible verse for devotion:

2 Thes. 3:6– When should fellowship be withdrawn?

Chapter 75

The Ordinances of the Church

Ordinances are those outward rites which Christ has appointed to be administered in His church as visible signs of the saving truth of the gospel.

- They are signs that vividly express the gospel to all.
- They are signs that confirm the gospel to believers.

It will be well to distinguish from one another the three words: Symbol, Rite, and Ordinance.

A *symbol* is the sign, or visible representation, of an invisible truth or idea. For example, the lion is the symbol of strength and courage, the lamb is the symbol of gentleness, the olive branch of peace, the scepter of dominion, the wedding ring of marriage, and the flag of country.

Symbols can teach great truths. Jesus' cursing the barren fig tree taught the doom of unfruitful Judaism. His washing of the disciples' feet taught His coming down from heaven to purify and save and the humble service He requires of us.

A *rite* is a symbol which is employed with regularity and sacred intent. Symbols became rites when thus used. Examples of common rites in the Christian church are the laying on of hands in ordination, and the giving of the right hand of fellowship.

An *ordinance* is a symbolic rite which sets forth the central truths of the Christian faith, and which is of universal and perpetual obligation. A church must observe these.

Baptism and the Lord's Supper are rites made ordinances by the commands of Christ. They both declare and remind us of the essential truths of His kingdom.

A *sacramentum* was the oath taken by the Roman soldier to obey his commander even unto death.

> *O Timothy, guard what has been entrusted to you, avoiding worldly and empty chatter and the opposing arguments of what is falsely called knowledge.*
> –1 Timothy 6:20

Baptism and the Lord's Supper are sacraments in the sense that they are vows of allegiance to Christ our Master.

No ordinance is a sacrament in the sense of conferring grace. They merely express and remind us of the grace of God already given. Salvation is by faith alone (Eph. 2:8-9).

In contrast with this characteristically Protestant view, Catholicism regards the ordinances as actually conferring grace and producing holiness. Instead of being the external manifestation of a preceding union with Christ, they are the physical means of constituting and maintaining this union. In this error, some Protestant churches substantially agree with Catholicism and are known as sacramentalists.

Catholicism holds to seven sacraments or ordinances: ordination, confirmation, matrimony, extreme unction, penance, baptism, and the Eucharist.

The ordinances prescribed in the New Testament, however, are two and only two: Baptism and the Lord's Supper. Both represent our union with Christ. They must be kept to proclaim the gospel and strengthen our faith.

Bible verse for devotion:

Mat. 5:19– Should we observe ordinances lightly?

Chapter 76

The Ordinance of Baptism

Baptism is symbolic of a believer's regeneration through union with Christ. The immersion of a believer in water is token of his previous entrance into the communion of Christ's death and resurrection.

- Baptism is a witness of Christ's death and resurrection.
- Baptism is to be observed only by believers.

Baptism witnesses to the world that Jesus died and rose again. It is a pictorial expression of the work of Christ. In Rom. 6:3-6, Paul wrote *"Or do you not know that all of us who have been baptized into Christ Jesus have been baptized into His death? Therefore we have been buried with Him through baptism into death, so that as Christ was raised from the dead through the glory of the Father, so we too might walk in newness of life. For if we have become united with Him in the likeness of His death, certainly we shall also be in the likeness of His resurrection, knowing this, that our old self was crucified with Him, in order that our body of sin might be done away with, so that we would no longer be slaves to sin."*

Baptism tells of the nature and penalty of sin (Rom. 6:3), of humanity delivered from sin in the Person of a crucified and risen Savior (Rom. 6:4), of salvation secured for each soul that is united to Christ (Rom. 6:5), and of obedience to Christ as the way to life and glory (Rom. 6:6). Thus baptism stands from age to age as a witness for God. In its symbol, we declare that Christ's death and resurrection has become ours.

Baptism was instituted by Christ and practiced by the apostles. In Mat. 28:19, Jesus says *"Go therefore and make disciples of all the nations, baptizing them in the name of the Father and the Son and the Holy Spirit."* In Acts 2:38, Peter says *"Repent, and each of you be baptized in the name of Jesus Christ for the forgiveness of your sins; and you will receive the gift of the Holy Spirit."*

> *But when they believed Philip preaching the good news about the kingdom of God and the name of Jesus Christ, they were being baptized, men and women alike.*
> **–Acts 8:12**

In His own submission to John's baptism, Christ gave testimony to the binding obligation of the ordinance (Mat. 3:13-17). He also demonstrated the proper mode of baptism, that being immersion. The baptism of Christ in the Jordan was by immersion to foreshadow His death and resurrection. Submersion and emergence are the very sense of the symbol.

John baptized upon profession of faith in a Savior yet to come (Acts 19:4). The significance of it was not understood in full until after Jesus' death and resurrection (Mat. 20:17-23; Luke 12:50; Rom. 6:3-6). Baptism is now administered upon profession of faith in a Savior who has actually and already come. It doesn't confer regeneration, but recognizes it (Acts 10:47). It is an act of obedience of the new believer.

To deny the observance of baptism, to change the mode of baptism, or to baptize unbelieving subjects is therefore to strike a blow at Christianity and at Christ, and to defraud the world of testimony to God's glorious salvation. Baptism is an indispensable witness to Christ's death and resurrection.

Bible verse for devotion:

Gal. 3:27–How are we incorporated into Christ?

Chapter 77

The Ordinance of the Lord's Supper

The Lord's Supper symbolizes the abiding communion of Christ's death and resurrection through which believers are sustained and perfected.

- It is a witness of Christ's death and resurrection.
- It is to be observed by an assembly of believers.

The church eats bread broken and drinks wine poured forth as a token of its constant dependence on the once crucified, now risen Savior, as source of its spiritual life.

1 Cor. 11:23-25, says *"For I received from the Lord that which I also delivered to you, that the Lord Jesus in the night in which He was betrayed took bread; and when He had given thanks, He broke it and said, This is My body, which is for you; do this in remembrance of Me. In the same way He took the cup also after supper, saying, This cup is the new covenant in My blood; do this, as often as you drink it, in remembrance of Me."*

The Lord's Supper and Baptism are both symbols of the death of Christ. In Baptism, we see Christ's death as the procuring cause of our new birth. In the Lord's Supper, we see Christ's death as the sustaining power of our new life.

The Lord's Supper doesn't confer new life, but celebrates it (Acts 2:42). The wine is the symbol of Christ's death. But it is His death by which we live. He drank the cup of suffering in order that we might drink the wine of joy. As broken bread sustains our life, Christ's broken body nourishes our soul.

The Lord's Supper was instituted by Christ and practiced by the apostles. Luke 22:19-20 records *"And when He had taken some bread and given thanks, He broke it and gave it to them, saying, This is My body which is given for you; do this in remembrance of Me. And in the same way He took the cup after they had eaten, saying, This cup which is poured out for you is the new covenant in My blood."*

> **For as often as you eat this bread and drink the cup, you proclaim the Lord's death until He comes.**
> **—1 Corinthians 11:26**

Christ commanded this ordinance to be observed by His disciples in remembrance of His death. This first Lord's Supper was Christian communion before Christ's death, just as John's baptism was Christian baptism before Christ's death. After His death, its role was realized (1 Cor. 11:26).

1 Cor. 11:27-34 is an exhortation for self-examination when taking the Lord's Supper. It is a call to recognize and appropriate the symbolism of the bread and wine. Thus, the Christian should not be deterred from participation by any feeling of his personal unworthiness, so long as he trusts Christ. The Lord's Supper testifies of His grace and mercy.

Gloom and sadness are foreign to the spirit of the Lord's Supper (Acts 2:46). It declares the life of Christ that sustains us. It symbolizes the coming joy and perfection of God's kingdom. In Mat. 26:29, Jesus promised *"I will not drink of this fruit of the vine from now on until that day when I drink it new with you in My Father's kingdom."* It brings before us, not simply death, but life; not simply past sacrifice but future glory. It points to our marriage supper (Rev. 19:9).

Bible verses for devotion:

1 Cor. 10:16-17—How is Christ incorporated into us?

X.   FINAL THINGS

Chapter 78

Physical Death

Physical death is the separation of the soul from the body. It is distinct from spiritual death, or separation of the soul from God. It is also distinct from the second death, or the banishment from God and final misery of the reunited soul and body of the wicked.

- Sinful man is spiritually dead, separated from God.
- Union with Christ by faith makes man alive again.

Scripture shows that death followed sin's entrance into the world. God warned Adam not to sin. In Gen. 2:17, God said "*... in the day that you eat from it you will surely die.*"

When Adam and Eve sinned, they died spiritually. They hid themselves from God (Gen. 3:8). They suffered the curse of pain and toil (Gen. 3:16-19). They were banished from the Garden of Eden and from the tree of life (Gen. 3:22-24).

In Gen. 3:22-23, God says "*Behold, the man has become like one of Us, knowing good and evil; and now, he might stretch out his hand, and take also from the tree of life, and eat, and live forever— therefore the LORD God sent him out of the garden of Eden to cultivate the ground...*"

Adam's soul was created in the image of the immortal God. Man had immortality of soul, and now, lest to this he add immortality of body, he is expelled from the tree of life.

Physical death now fell upon humanity as the penalty of sin (James 1:15). In sin, man is corrupted, both body and soul.

In spiritual death, the soul is separated from God. In physical death, the soul is separated from body. God promises a resurrection of body for the just and unjust.

> *Therefore there is now no condemnation for those who are in Christ Jesus. For the law of the Spirit of life in Christ Jesus has set you free from the law of sin and of death.*
> **–Romans 8:1-2**

For all who are in Christ, physical death loses its penal aspect and becomes entrance into life eternal with God. Psalm 116:15 says *"Precious in the sight of the Lord is the death of His godly ones."* Because of our union with Christ, we will share in His resurrection. In this hope, Paul triumphantly wrote *"O Death, where is your victory? O Death, where is your sting?"* (1 Cor. 15:55).

As there is a life beyond the present life for the faithful, so there is death beyond death for the wicked. Death begins here, but culminates hereafter.

Body and soul are reunited in conscious separation from God. Their part is a *"...lake that burns with fire and brimstone, which is the second death"* (Rev. 21:8). This is but a continuance of spiritual death for all of eternity.

The just will *"...not be hurt by the second death"* (Rev. 2:11). The unjust has but *"...wrath to come"* (Mat. 3:7). *"He is not the God of the dead but of the living"* (Mat. 22:32).

In 2 Tim. 1:10, Paul exalts *"...our Savior Christ Jesus, who abolished death and brought life and immortality to light through the gospel."* The gospel promises eternal life. Christ's resurrection carries with it our own resurrection.

Bible verse for devotion:

James 5:20– How can you save others from death?

Chapter 79

The Intermediate State

The Scriptures affirm the conscious existence of both the righteous and the wicked, after death, and prior to the resurrection. In the intermediate state, the soul is without a body. The righteous experience a conscious joy. The wicked experience a conscious suffering.

- The resurrection of the body is future, not immediate.
- Neither the just nor unjust are unconscious in this state.

That believers do not receive the spiritual body at death is plain from 1 Thes. 4:16-17 and 1 Cor. 15:52, where an interval is intimated between Paul's time and the rising of those who slept. This rising is to occur in the future, *"at the last trump."* Likewise, the coinciding resurrection of the wicked is also described as future (Jn. 5:28-29; Acts 24:15).

The soul of the believer, at its separation from the body, enters the presence of Christ. In Luke 23:43, Jesus assured the criminal *"...today you shall be with Me in Paradise."*

Paradise is none other than the abode of God and the rest and blessedness of the saints (Rev. 6:9-11; Rev. 14:13). Paul wrote of his desire for God over earth. Phil. 1:23 says *"But I am hard-pressed from both directions, having the desire to depart and be with Christ, for that is very much better."*

The wicked at death enter a state of constraint and guard (1 Pet. 3:19), torment and conscious suffering (Luke 16:23), and are kept *"...under punishment for the day of judgment"* (2 Pet. 2:9). They await judgment and the second death.

The departed are described as "spirits" (Eccl. 12:7; Acts 7:59; Heb. 12:23; 1 Pet. 3:19). But this is not inconsistent with their conscious activity as described in Scripture.

> *We are of good courage, I say, and prefer rather to be absent from the body and to be at home with the Lord.*
> **–2 Corinthians 5:8**

When the dead are spoken of as "sleeping" (Dan. 12:2; Mat. 9:24; Jn. 11:11; 1 Cor. 11:30; 15:51; 1 Thes. 4:14; 5:10), we are to regard this as simply the language of appearance, and as literally applicable only to the body.

The Roman Catholic doctrine of Purgatory is without Scriptural warrant. They erroneously teach that in the intermediate state, believers make satisfaction for the sins committed after baptism by suffering according to their guilt.

Purgatory is inconsistent with any proper view of the completeness of Christ's satisfaction (Gal. 2:21; Heb. 9:28); of justification through faith alone (Rom. 3:28); and of the condition after death, of both the righteous and wicked, as determined in this life (Eccl. 11:3; Mat. 25:10; Luke 16:26; Heb. 9:27; Rev. 22:11). The true purgatory is only in this world, for only here are sins purged away in sanctification by the Holy Spirit. In this, there is never an element of penalty.

While the Scriptures represent the intermediate state to be one of conscious joy to the righteous, and of conscious pain to the wicked, they also represent this state to be one of incompleteness (Mat. 8:29; 2 Pet. 2:9; Rev. 6:10). The perfect joy of the saints, and the utter misery of the wicked, begin only with the resurrection and general judgment.

Bible verse for devotion:

1 Thes. 5:10– Who do we abide with in life or death?

Chapter 80

The Second Coming of Christ

Christ will triumphantly return to punish the wicked and to gather His people to Him and glorify them.

- The second coming of Christ will be literal and visible.
- No one knows the time of His triumphant return.

In Old Testament prophecy, divine interference in man's affairs are often represented under the figure of God coming in the clouds (Ps. 104:3-4; Zeph. 1:14-15; Jer. 4:28-29).

In the New Testament, great events in the history of the individual Christian, like death (Jn. 14:3), and great events in the history of the church, like the outpouring of the Spirit at Pentecost (Jn. 14:18) and the destruction of Jerusalem (Mat. 24:34), are represented as comings of Christ for deliverance or judgment. These are but preliminary and typical comings.

Scripture declares that these partial and typical comings will be concluded by a final coming of Christ. His return will be the entire submission of the will of man to the will of God.

Christ's return will not be subjective and spiritual. It will constitute a visible, bodily manifestation of God like that of His first coming (Acts 1:11), but unspeakably more glorious.

Mat. 25:31-32 states *"But when the Son of Man comes in His glory, and all the angels with Him, then He will sit on His glorious throne. All the nations will be gathered before Him; and He will separate them from one another, as the shepherd separates the sheep from the goats."*

2 Thes. 1:7-10 says Christ's coming will *"...give relief to you who are afflicted and to us as well when the Lord Jesus will be revealed from heaven with His mighty angels in flaming fire, dealing out retribution to those who do not know God and to those who do not obey the gospel of our Lord Jesus. These will pay the penalty of eternal destruction, away from the presence of the Lord and from the glory of His power, when He comes to be glorified in His saints on that day, and to be marveled at among all who have believed..."*

> *For the Son of Man is going to come in the glory of His Father with His angels, and will then repay every man according to his deeds.*
> **–Matthew 16:27**

Early Christians seem to have hoped for this occurrence during their lifetime. Yet neither Christ nor His apostles definitely taught when the end would be, but rather reserved the knowledge of it to the counsels of God (Mk. 13:32; Acts 1:7). Thus, we must live as it is possibly at hand and so ever be in its hope (2 Tim. 4:8; Ja. 5:7-8; 1 Pet. 4:7; 2 Pet. 3:13).

Scripture warns us of deceivers and mockers who will deny Christ's return (2 John 1:7; 2 Pet. 3:3-13). We are to be steadfast and remember God's grace in that *"The Lord is not slow about His promise, as some count slowness, but is patient toward you, not wishing for any to perish but for all to come to repentance"* (2 Pet. 3:9).

Christ will come to put an end to the world's long sorrow, to give triumph to the cause of truth, and to reward His own. His glory will be finally revealed in us (Col. 3:4; Rom. 8:18).

Bible verse for devotion:

Luke 18:8– Will Christ find faith, at least in us?

Chapter 81

The Resurrection

At the second coming of Christ, there will be a resurrection of the body for the just and the unjust. It is a reunion of the body to the soul from which it has been separated during the intermediate state.

- The just will be resurrected to life in a body like Christ's.
- The unjust will be a resurrected to eternal condemnation.

While the Scriptures describe the impartation of new life to the soul in regeneration as a spiritual resurrection, they also declare that there will be a resurrection of the body.

In Acts 24:15, Paul told Felix that *"...there shall certainly be a resurrection of both the righteous and the wicked."* The book of Revelation describes this resurrection. Rev. 20:13 says *"...the sea gave up the dead which were in it, and death and Hades gave up the dead which were in them; and they were judged, every one of them according to their deeds."*

Rom. 8:11 says *"...if the Spirit of Him who raised Jesus from the dead dwells in you, He who raised Christ from the dead will also give life to your mortal bodies through His Spirit who dwells in you."* God renews us, body and soul.

Phil. 3:20-21 states *"For our citizenship is in heaven, from which we also eagerly wait for the Savior, the Lord Jesus Christ, who will transform the body of our humble state into conformity with the body of His glory, by the exertion of the power that He has even to subject all things to Himself."* He will resurrect and glorify us on that day.

It is not by acting upon the bride of Christ from without, but by energizing it from within, that the Holy Spirit will effect its glorification. The Comforter, who came down at Pentecost to form a spiritual body out of flesh, will at the Second Coming return to heaven in that body, having fashioned it like unto the body of Christ.

> *Do not marvel at this; for an hour is coming, in which all who are in the tombs will hear His voice, and will come forth; those who did the good deeds to a resurrection of life, those who committed the evil deeds to a resurrection of judgment.*
> **–John 5:28-29**

Those who are living at Christ's coming shall receive spiritual bodies without passing through death. Paul promises in 1 Cor. 15:51-54, *"Behold, I tell you a mystery; we will not all sleep, but we will all be changed, in a moment, in the twinkling of an eye, at the last trumpet; for the trumpet will sound, and the dead will be raised imperishable, and we will be changed. For this perishable must put on the imperishable, and this mortal must put on immortality. But when this perishable will have put on the imperishable, and this mortal will have put on immortality, then will come about the saying that is written, Death is swallowed up in victory."* Because Christ's resurrection is ours, *"...we shall always be with the Lord"* (1 Thes. 4:17).

As the body after corruption and dissolution, so the outward world after destruction by fire, will be rehabilitated and fit for our abode (Rom. 8:20-22; Phil. 3:20; Rev. 21:5).

Bible verses for devotion:

Mat. 17:1-9– How is this a prophecy of resurrection?

Chapter 82

The Last Judgment

The Last Judgment is the final and complete vindication of God's righteousness. The characters of all men will be made known to the universe, and they will be awarded their corresponding destinies.

- All people will be gathered for judgment at His coming.
- The bodies of the dead will be resurrected for judgment.

While Scripture ascribes all earthly punishment of the wicked as acts of judgment, it also intimates that these are, partial, imperfect, and incomplete. God will vindicate His justice in a definite, outward and visible day of judgment. On that day, all men will be judged by Christ (Jn. 5:22, 27).

In Acts 17:31, Paul declared *"...He has fixed a day in which He will judge the world in righteousness through a Man whom He has appointed, having furnished proof to all men by raising Him from the dead."*

Judgment is something for which the evil are kept (2 Pet. 2:4, 9); something expected in the future (Acts 24:25; Heb. 10:27); something after death (Heb. 9:27); and something for which the resurrection is a preparation (John 5:29).

The object of the final judgment is not the ascertainment, but the manifestation, of character, and the assignment of outward condition corresponding to it. To the omniscient Judge, the condition of all moral creatures is already and fully known. The last day will be but the *"...revelation of the righteous judgment of God"* (Rom. 2:5-6; 1 Tim. 5:24-25).

The grounds of the final judgment will be twofold.

Its first ground is the law of God (Rom. 2:12-13). This is revealed in conscience and Scripture. In Jn. 12:48, Jesus said *"He who rejects Me and does not receive My sayings, has one who judges him; the word that I spoke is what will judge him at the last day."* Jesus Christ is both Judge and the Word by which He judges.

> *For we must all appear before the judgment seat of Christ, so that each one may be recompensed for his deeds in the body, according to what he has done, whether good or bad.*
> **—2 Corinthians 5:10**

The second ground of the final judgment is the grace of Christ (Rom. 3:20-21). By God's infinite grace, He gives *"even the righteousness of God through faith in Jesus Christ for all those who believe"* (Rom. 3:22).

Rev. 20:12 states *"And I saw the dead, the great and the small, standing before the throne, and books were opened; and another book was opened, which is the book of life; and the dead were judged from the things which were written in the books, according to their deeds."* The *"books"* opened are books of condemnation, in which are written the names of those who stand in their sins. They are unrepentant and unforgiven. The *"book of life"* is the book of justification, in which is written every name that is united to Christ by faith.

Judgment will be an unmixed blessing to the just. There is no fear in the words *"Prepare to meet your God"*, for He is their *"Prince and a Savior"* (Amos 4:12; Acts 5:31). *"Let us rejoice and be glad and give the glory to Him..."* (Rev. 19:7).

Bible verses for devotion:

John 3:18-21– Have you come to the light?

Chapter 83

The Final State of the Wicked

The final state of the wicked is the loss of all good and the misery of an evil conscience banished from God and the just, and forever under God's positive curse.

- Hell is the absence of God's graceful presence.
- Hell is the manifestation of God's wrathful presence.

In our study of man's fall, we saw that penalty is the necessary reaction of the holiness of God against sin. Penalty is the vindication of the character of the Lawgiver (Gal. 6:7-8). The penalty of sin is death. Hell, or the second death, may be regarded as the culmination and completion of penalty.

The final state of the wicked is described alternatively as eternal fire (Mat. 25:41), the pit of the abyss (Rev. 9:2, 11), outer darkness (Mat. 8:12), torment (Rev. 14:10-11), eternal punishment (Mat. 25:46), the wrath of God (Rom. 2:5), second death (Rev. 21:8), eternal destruction from the face of the Lord (2 Thes. 1:9), and even eternal sin (Mark 3:29).

For the wicked, death is not a cessation of being (Mat. 25:46). The wicked at death enter a state of conscious suffering. As the soul is immortal, its punishment is forever.

Everlasting punishment of the wicked is not inconsistent with God's justice, but is rather a revelation of that justice. Punishment cannot come to an end until guilt and sin come to an end. But guilt is endless. And so is sin, for sin is not an act only, but also a condition or state of the soul (Mark 3:29; Rev. 22:11). Thus, punishment is as endless as its reasons.

We must remember that men are finally condemned, not merely for sins, but for sin. They are punished for their evil character.

The soul that is unlike God cannot dwell with God (Luke 16:26; Rev. 22:15). Sin is self-isolating. The misery of the wicked hereafter will doubtless

> *These will pay the penalty of eternal destruction, away from the presence of the Lord and from the glory of His power.*
> **–2 Thes. 1:9**

be due in part to their evil company. The judgment is but a remanding of men to their "...*own place*" (Acts 1:25).

Hell is a finite place. It is a '*pit*,' a '*lake*'; not an ocean. It is '*bottomless*', not boundless. But there is no limit to the suffering there. They are "...*in the lake that burns with fire and brimstone, which is the second death*" (Rev. 21:8).

In Hell, there may be degrees of penalty in God's administration based on one's earthly works (Luke 12:47-48; Rom. 2:5-6; 2 Cor. 5:10; 2 Cor. 11:15; 2 Tim. 4:14; Rev. 2:23; Rev. 18:5-6). For certain, the wicked will not be in God's gracious presence, but in His wrathful presence (Heb. 10:31).

We must never deny or ignore the doctrine of eternal punishment. To do so is to be similar to Satan, when he told Eve "*You surely will not die*" (Gen. 3:4). The most fearful utterances of future punishment are those of Jesus Himself (Mat. 10:28; Mat. 23:33; Mat. 25:46; Mark 3:29).

We know the enormity of sin only by God's own declarations with regard to it, and by the sacrifice which He has made to redeem us from it. Hell, as well as the Cross, indicates God's estimate of sin. The Cross shows His love.

Bible verses for devotion:

Luke 12:4-5– Of what does Jesus warn us?

Chapter 84

The Final State of the Righteous

The final state of the righteous is the fullness and perfection of holy life, in eternal communion with God and with sanctified spirits.

- Heaven is a state of perfect communion with God.
- Heaven is also the community of the redeemed of God.

The final state of the righteous is described as eternal life (Mat. 25:46), glory (2 Cor. 4:17), rest (Heb. 4:9), knowledge (1 Cor. 13:8-10), holiness (Rev. 21:27), service (Rev. 22:3), worship (Rev. 19:1), society (Heb. 12:23), and communion with God (Rev. 21:3). This blessed state will be unchanging in kind and endless in duration (Rev. 3:12; 22:15).

Heaven will involve deliverance from death, sorrow, and pain (Rev. 21:4), from fallen surroundings (Rev. 21:1), as well as from the remains of evil in our hearts (Rev. 21:5). We will be perfect as we enter Heaven, free from sin (Rev. 21:27). We will be free from curse (Rev. 22:3) and darkness (Rev. 22:5).

We shall also be perfect in the sense of knowing God. In 1 Cor. 13:12, Paul said *"For now we see in a mirror, dimly, but then face to face; now I know in part, but then I will know fully just as I also have been fully known."*

Heaven is more than just a state. It is deemed an actual place (Jn. 14:2; Rev. 21:2). Heaven described as a city seems to suggest security from every foe (Rev. 21:17), provision for every want (Rev. 22:2), intensity of life and occupations (Rev. 21:25), and closeness of relation to others (Rev. 21:24).

Rest, in Heaven, will be consistent with service. It will be a holy activity without weariness, a service of perfect joy and freedom.

On earth, the greatest degradation and sin are found in the great cities. In Heaven, the life of the city will only help holiness and service, as the life of the city here below helps wickedness.

> *But just as it is written: Things which eye has not seen and ear has not heard, and which have entered the heart of man, all that God has prepared for those who love Him.*
> **–1 Corinthians 2:9**

Brotherly love on earth implies knowing those we love, and loving those we know. If we know our friends here, we will know them in Heaven as well. We certainly will not know less in Heaven than here. And, as love to Christ here draws us nearer to each other, so there we shall love friends, not less but more, because of our greater nearness to Christ.

In Heaven, there may be degrees of blessedness and honor, proportioned to the capacity and fidelity of every person in their earthly works (Luke 19:17, 19; 1 Cor. 3:14-15). For certain, all the redeemed will receive as great a measure of reward as they can contain (1 Cor. 2:9).

Our greatest reward will be God Himself. Rev. 21:3 says *"And I heard a loud voice from the throne, saying, Behold, the tabernacle of God is among men, and He will dwell among them, and they shall be His people, and God Himself will be among them."* Jesus promised *"If I go and prepare a place for you, I will come again and receive you to Myself, that where I am, there you may be also"* (Jn. 14:3).

Bible verses for devotion:

Heb. 12:14, 28-29– What should we follow after?

Made in the USA
San Bernardino, CA
22 September 2014